T0300419

Agrarian Change in Egypt

First published in 1986, *Agrarian Change in Egypt* based on extensive original research as well as field survey of eighteen villages, analyses and explains the changes in the agricultural sector in Egypt. It shows how various policies and other factors have affected agricultural output and how developments triggered by the 'open door policy' such as inflation, migration, and the shift in the pricing system have affected agriculture. The Egyptian experience is fairly typical of agrarian change in many parts of the developing world where government reforms in the 1960s and 1970s tried to combine considerations of efficiency and equity but ended up with stagnation. The Egyptian case therefore provides a good example of the general crisis in agriculture in the developing world. This book is an essential read for scholars and researchers of agricultural economy, development studies and political economy.

Agrarian Change in Egypt

An Anatomy of Rural Poverty

Samir Radwan and Eddy Lee

Routledge
Taylor & Francis Group

First published in 1986
by Croom Helm

This edition first published in 2022 by Routledge
4 Park Square, Milton Park, Abingdon, Oxon, OX14 4RN

and by Routledge
605 Third Avenue, New York, NY 10017

Routledge is an imprint of the Taylor & Francis Group, an informa business

Publisher's Note
The publisher has gone to great lengths to ensure the quality of this reprint but points
out that some imperfections in the original copies may be apparent.

Disclaimer
The publisher has made every effort to trace copyright holders and welcomes
correspondence from those they have been unable to contact.

A Library of Congress record exists under ISBN: 0709942141

ISBN: 978-1-032-32214-8 (hbk)
ISBN: 978-1-003-31341-0 (ebk)
ISBN: 978-1-032-32215-5 (pbk)

Book DOI 10.4324/9781003313410

AGRARIAN CHANGE in EGYPT

AN ANATOMY OF RURAL POVERTY

Samir Radwan
and
Eddy Lee

A study prepared for the International Labour Office
within the framework of the World Employment Programme

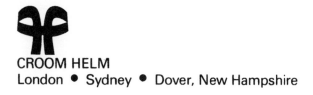

CROOM HELM
London • Sydney • Dover, New Hampshire

Copyright © International Labour Organisation 1986
Croom Helm Ltd, Provident House, Burrell Row,
Beckenham, Kent BR3 1AT
Croom Helm Australia Pty Ltd, Suite 4, 6th Floor, 64-76 Kippax Street,
Surry Hills, NSW 2010, Australia

British Library Cataloguing in Publication Data

Radwan, Samir
   Agrarian change in Egypt: an anatomy of
   rural poverty.
   1. Egypt—Rural conditions 2. Egypt—
   Economic conditions—1962-
   I. Title II. Lee, Eddy III. International
   Labour Office   IV. World Employment Programme
   330.962   HC830
Croom Helm, 51, Washington Street, Dover,
New Hampshire 03820,USA

Library of Congress Cataloging in Publication Data

Radwan, Samir Muhammad
   Agrarian change in Egypt
   A study prepared for the International Labour Office
   within the framework of the World Employment Programme.
   includes index.
   1. Egypt—Rural Conditions   2. Poor—Egypt   3. Agriculture—
   Economic aspects—Egypt   I. Lee, Eddy   II. World Employment
   Programme   III. Title.
   HN786.A8R33 1985   305.6'69'0962   85-11356
   ISBN 0-7099-4214-1

Printed and bound in Great Britain by Mackays of Chatham Ltd, Kent

Contents

Figures

Tables

Acknowledgements

This work was only possible through the collaboration and help of numerous individuals and institutes. Our thanks go primarily to the team of the Institute of National Planning in Cairo under the competent leadership of Dr M.A. Mongy. This team shouldered the major responsibility of carrying out the field survey, and Dr Mongy was closely associated with the writing up of the manuscript. Dr Ismail Sabry Abdullah, then Minister of Planning and Director of the INP, gave unfailing support to the project.

We would like to extend our thanks to the Federal Republic of Germany, who financed the survey work under their multi-bilateral programme with the ILO.

At the ILO Messrs Dharam Ghai, A. R. Khan, Gerry Rodgers, Peter Richards, William Keddeman and Guy Standing commented on various versions of the manuscript. Our special thanks go to Mr A. Wagner, whose help in data processing and tabulation was invaluable. Mrs Kristina Boudjenane gave generously of her time in the processing and tabulation of data.

In finalising the manuscript Mr Adel Sadek of the University of Oxford was most helpful in providing counter arguments and material for updating the last chapter. His assistance is warmly acknowledged. Dr. Hamid Tabatabai was most helpful in revising the draft.

Finally, thanks to Sandra Deacon, Lesley Brooks, Geraldine Ople and Terry Powell for typing successive versions of this manuscript with unfailing care and dedication.

Samir Radwan and Eddy Lee

1 Introduction

As the title suggests, rather than being a pure country study, this book is mainly focused on the anatomy of rural poverty as reflected in the case of Egypt. Thus we have the twin objective of developing a methodology for the analysis of poverty in a poor agrarian economy and illustrating the scope and limitations of this methodology by reference to the experience of Egypt over the last quarter of a century.[1] The study is primarily centred around the results of a survey of a random sample of 1,000 households in 18 villages in Egypt carried out in February 1977. The survey was especially designed in such a way as to obtain the data required for the empirical analysis of the dimensions, nature and causes of poverty in an agrarian economy. The data thus generated are used to test a number of hypotheses and relationships central to the study of agrarian change. Thus the household questionnaire was designed to elicit information on the major correlates of rural poverty: land distribution and changes therein, employment characteristics of the rural households, levels of wages and the functioning of the labour market in a land-scarce, densely populated economy, the distribution of productive assets, consumption and access to services. One of the important inter-relationships investigated is the relationship between poverty and ownership of productive assets, and between poverty and various sources of income. An important hypothesis to be tested is the extent to which the lack of access to productive assets, especially land, explains rural poverty. Equally important is the hypothesis about the importance of wage-employment as a source of income in an agrarian economy with an unfavourable land/man ratio. A novel feature of this approach is the attempt to trace the movements in land ownership during the lifetime of the household members. As will be seen, the pressure of population growth in a land-scarce economy has been borne mainly by the small farmers. One can speak of a process of marginal-isation in the sense that farmers in the lower land ownership groups have been losing their land and joining the ranks of the landless. A corollary of this phenomenon is the pattern of employment in such an economy. As will be demonstrated, a substantial proportion of the rural labour force has to find employment outside the agricultural sector. Given the narrowness of the rural market, rural non-agricultural activities are not highly developed. Given also the difficulty of finding renumerative employment opportunities in the congested urban areas, we found that a sizeable proportion of rural labour is 'trapped' in the villages and has to eke out a living by engaging in handicrafts and petty trade, or what we call the tertiarisation of the rural areas.

The study, however, goes beyond a mere quantitative analysis of the survey results. It draws upon a wide range of other primary and secondary data to analyse the dynamics of agrarian change in Egypt over the last three decades.

Egypt provides an extremely illustrative example of that group of countries which attempted to effect agrarian transition through a major institutional change. The most important instrument of this change is the reform of the old land tenure system based on private land ownership and the creation of an alternative form of organisation believed to be more conducive to egalitarian rural development – thus the significance of the developments witnessed over the last quarter of a century in rural Egypt: successive agrarian reforms, co-operative organisation and the introduction of a wide range of public policies affecting marketing, pricing and investment.

Many surveys and studies have been concerned with the evaluation of these developments. By and large, the focus has been on one or the other of the following areas:

(i)   The impact of various development programmes and government policies on the *growth* of agricultural output. Here attempts were made to assess the impact on agricultural output of the two major policy packages: 'horizontal expansion', i.e. expansion of arable land through irrigation and land-reclamation projects; and 'vertical expansion', i.e. increasing the productivity of land under cultivation through technical progress. Underlying all these studies was the assumption that rural development meant a rapid rate of growth of agricultural output.

(ii)   The effect of land reform on rural Egypt. The emphasis here was placed on describing the objectives of such a reform and the legal and institutional framework thereby introduced. Very few studies, however, have concerned themselves with serious assessment of the actual impact agrarian reform had on rural Egypt. Even these stress the implications of the new reform on land ownership and land tenure.

(iii) Problems of labour utilisation in the agricultural sector. This is one of the most thoroughly researched aspects of rural Egypt. A major survey of rural employment problems was carried out in 1964/5 by the ILO and the Institute of National Planning, the results of which were published in 1969.[2] The survey mapped out the employment situation, quantified rural under-development and unemployment and briefly assessed the impact of development policy on rural labour. The results of the survey (together with the various studies using its output) have no doubt provided a base of hard data on the question of labour utilisation in rural Egypt. The main weakness of the survey, however, was the very limited and superficial coverage of aspects related to wages, incomes and consumption in rural areas (Report C of the background papers.)

It is clear from the brief survey presented above that little or no concern was in fact given to the assessment of the impact of various development policies on income distribution and social stratification, the transformation of the agrarian structure, the conditions affecting the performance of the agricultural sector and the place of that sector within the wider framework of the economy as a whole. Moreover, no attempt was made to study the problem of rural poverty, the most constant feature of the Egyptian village since the Pharaohs. A number of fragmentary studies which purported to map out the income distribution situation were based exclusively on the results of two Family Budget Surveys (of 1958/9 and 1964/5) as well as the latest agricultural census of 1961.[3] These studies had, therefore, all the inherent limitations of attempting to establish an income distribution matrix solely from consumption-expenditure data. The data base of these studies relates only to the 1960s and therefore it fails to reflect some of the significant changes that have taken place since then. An agricultural census scheduled for 1970/1 was never carried out, hence the severe constraint on any serious analysis of recent developments.

In view of these limitations on our knowledge of conditions in rural Egypt and the urgent need to help in the process of policy formulation (at present the subject of an extremely lively debate), it was necessary to carry out the survey mentioned above. The purpose was threefold: (a) to provide up-to-date data on various aspects of development in rural Egypt; (b) to evaluate the impact of different policies on the agricultural sector in general and the rural poor in particular; and (c) to deduce the policy implications of the present situation. The orientation of the present study is, therefore, different from previous efforts. The focus is on issues of poverty, inequality and the conditions of employment in a poor agrarian economy.

To achieve these objectives Chapter 2 provides a brief historical background to the pre-land reform developments of the Egyptian agrarian system to set the scene for the evaluation of subsequent developments. In this chapter the methodology used in the survey is also briefly explained. The subsequent three chapters draw on the results of the survey in an attempt to evaluate the performance of the rural economy in three vital aspects. Thus Chapter 3 provides an analysis of the generation and distribution of income in rural Egypt. Chapter 4 analyses the structure of asset ownership and investigates the inter-relationship between asset holding and poverty on the one hand and agricultural production on the other. Chapter 5 focuses on the problem of rural poverty in an attempt to provide an anatomy of this problem by measuring the dimensions of the problem, trying to identify the major correlates of poverty and outlining the nature of the life of the poor in rural Egypt. The study also provides (Chapter 6) an analysis of the problem of employment and the functioning of the labour market. In this chapter three major issues are discussed: the pattern of rural employment and labour utilisation, the determinants of wages in a poor agrarian economy, and the factors affecting labour supply in such an economy. Finally, in Chapter 7 an attempt will be made to contrast the picture of the agrarian structure of the 1970s that emerged from the previous chapters with the subsequent developments that took place during the late 1970s and early 1980s. The period covered by the present survey represents a watershed, since it witnessed major changes that were to shape the agrarian structure in the 1980s, yet the full effect of these changes was to be felt only by the turn of the decade.

Notes

1. The present study is part of a broader attempt to develop the methodology of measuring the magnitude of poverty and analysing its attributes and causes. The approach to data collection was outlined in Samir Radwan and Torkel Alfthan: 'Household surveys for basic needs: Some issues', in *International Labour Review* (Geneva, ILO), March-April 1978. This approach has been applied to the United Republic of Tanzania and Sri Lanka as well as Egypt.

2. ILO: *Rural employment problems in the United Arab Republic* (Geneva, 1969). See also the study based on this survey: B. Hansen: 'Employment and wages in rural Egypt', in *American Economic Review*, June 1969; and the study by Amr Mohie-Eldine: 'Employment problems and policies in Egypt', paper presented to the ILO/ECWA Seminar on Manpower and Employment Planning in the Arab Countries, Beirut, 1975, published in ILO: *Manpower and employment in Arab countries: Some selected issues* (Geneva, 1976).

3. The only studies available are M. Abdel-Fadil: *Development, income distribution and social change in rural Egypt (1952-1970)*, Occasional Paper No. 45 (University of Cambridge, Department of Applied Economics, 1975); and S. Radwan: *Agrarian reform and rural development: Egypt 1952-1975* (Geneva, ILO, 1977).

2 Background and Methodology

Introduction

It is essential at the outset of this study to provide a historical and methodological background in order to put into proper perspective the detailed results obtained from the survey of rural Egypt. This chapter will thus begin with a brief outline of the evolution of Egypt's agrarian system in order to place into historical perspective the realities of the situation as they emerge from the survey results and to promote an understanding of the major problems of Egyptian agriculture. Secondly, an attempt will be made to contrast these realities with the various writings which tried to analyse the 'agrarian question' in that country. Finally, a summary review of the methodology used will be presented with a view to highlighting its broad features and rationale.

The Evolution of Egypt's Agrarian System: a Brief Historical Background

The Situation at Mid-century

Egypt's agrarian system of the 1950s had its historical roots in the system of private land ownership, established in the second half of the nineteenth century, and the concomitant emergence of a powerful class of large landowners.[1] The most striking feature which characterised the evolution of this system was the heavy concentration of land ownership on the one hand, and the continued fragmentation of small landholdings on the other. An initial situation of extreme inequality in the distribution of land had actually worsened with the passage of time. Thus we find that at the turn of the century small farmers (owning less than 5 feddans), who represented 80 per cent of the total number of landowners, possessed only 20 per cent of the land, while large proprietors (owning over 50 feddans), representing only 1.5 per cent of landowners, held 44 per cent of the land.[2] The process of differentiation continued. Thus, through the parallel processes of fragmentation of small properties and consolidation of medium and large properties, the distribution of land ownership, extremely uneven from the beginning, became even more

6

unequal. The Gini coefficient for the distribution of land ownership increased from 0.696 in 1896 to 0.785 in 1950. Consequently, we find that on the eve of the First Agrarian Reform of 1952 large landlords, owning over 50 feddans, numbered less than half of 1 per cent of the total number of proprietors but held 35 per cent of the land, while, at the other end of the spectrum, small farmers, owning less than 1 feddan, represented 72 per cent of total landowners but held only 13 per cent of the land. It is not surprising, therefore, that Egypt was then described as the 'half per cent society'. The 2 million families which owned less than 1 feddan each constituted the poorest section of the landowning class; some, having leased their land to other peasants, lived in towns or joined the army of casual labourers in the villages; others rented land to supplement their holdings whenever possible.[3]

Land rent (involving as much as 60 per cent of the cultivated land in the 1950s) may be regarded as a means of ensuring access of the landless to land, and thus might have improved land distribution. A comparison of the size-distribution of *landholdings* with that of *land ownerships* brought out quite clearly that 'one of the basic features of the land tenure system in Egypt is the tendency to concentrate the land into larger holdings than the freeholds'.[4] Thus, the economic function of tenancy was 'to break up large ownerships and consolidate very small parcels into holdings of operational size.[5]

Outside the spectrum of landowners we find the landless peasants, the poorest of the rural poor. With no access to land either through ownership or rent, the number of landless families, as well as their proportion to total rural population, has been growing considerably. In 1929 there were 697,000 landless families, or 37 per cent of the rural households. The ratio increased to 53 per cent in 1939, and by 1950 there were some 1.5 million families, representing 60 per cent of rural population, which neither owned nor rented land at all and which had to rely exclusively on their labour for earning a living.[6]

The Agrarian Reform and its Impact

It is against this background that a number of writers, social reformers and politicians called for the reform of the agrarian system.[7] Various elaborate schemes were proposed, but all went unheeded. One of the first actions of the 1952 Revolution was the promulgation of the Land Reform Law of September 1952, which represented a frontal attack on the power of the entrenched class of big landowners and an attempt at a radical reform of an ailing agrarian system.

The first and perhaps most important point to note was that the land reform of 1952 and subsequent measure in 1961 and 1969 did not result in the total upheaval of the old system. In fact, this was not one of the aims of this reform; its major objective was to break the power of large landowners and raise the standard of living of the peasantry through the enforcement of complementary measures such as tenancy reforms and minimum wage legislation within the framework of private land ownership.

The tenancy and minimum wage reforms had a potentially wider redistributive impact. At the time of land reform 60 per cent of the total land area was tenant-cultivated and an estimated 60 per cent of rural families were landless and hence dependent, to varying degrees, on income from agricultural wages. The number of potential beneficiaries from these measures was thus very great. The 1952 Land Reform Law fixed rents at seven times the land tax in case of cash tenancy and, in the case of share-cropping, the tenants' share in the crop was set at 50 per cent, with equal participation in costs between owner and tenant. Security of tenure was also guaranteed for three years. The impact of these measures, fully applied, could have lowered the level of cash rents by 30 to 42 per cent [8] and brought about an increase of one-third in the share of total output retained by share-croppers. Similarly, the minimum wage for an eight-hour day was set at 18 piastres for men and 10 piastres for women compared with the prevailing rates of 10-15 piastres and 6-7 piastres respectively.

Undoubtedly, there was a significant initial redistribution as a result of these measures, but the enforcement of rent control and minimum wage legislation was patchy and evasion was widespread. The strong demand for land and the domination of land reform institutions by large landowners made it easy to continue squeezing peasants. In addition, under conditions of growing population pressure, many landlords have succeeded in evading the minimum wage stipulations and, as we show in the next section, there has been no sustained improvement in real wages.

Thus, neither the redistribution of land itself nor the accompanying tenancy and wage reforms had any radical effect in changing the agrarian system. There were some initial, once-and-for-all gains in asset and income redistribution but these were, as we shall show, eroded away as the system reverted to a new inegalitarian equilibrium. The post-reform system was still based on the private ownership of land and the redistribution of land remained highly unequal; the top 5.6 per cent of landowning households still owned 53.4 per cent of the total cultivated area after the 1952 reform. The vast majority of the landowning population (94.4 per cent) owned only 46.6 per cent of total cultivated land and owned an average of 1 feddan per owner; in contrast, 20 per cent of the total area was in ownership units of more than 50 feddans and another 14 per cent was in units of between 20 and 50 feddans. Thus, the range in the size of ownership units still remained enormous in spite of the elimination of the top of the landowning pyramid through the 1952 reform.

Furthermore, a large pool of landless families continued to exist. No less than 40 per cent of agricultural families were still estimated to be landless after the land reform.[9]

Because land continued to be highly unequally distributed and a large pool of landless peasants continued to exist, it is clear that the structural conditions for the perpetuation and deepening of rural poverty were not drastically weakened. Unequal land ownership confers monopsonistic power in labour markets against a large and powerless rural labour reserve.[10] Market power also extends to the supply of credit and economic control by the rich of the poor through usurious relationships. Moreover, political power, as a result of the land reform, had merely shifted from the very rich to the rich; the political position of the mass of the rural poor remained unchanged.

Another distinctive feature of the post-reform agrarian system, and one that is perhaps unique to the Egyptian case (as well as the case of Mexican Eijidos), was the introduction of the system of 'supervised co-operatives'. The First Agrarian Reform of 1952 made it obligatory for all land reform beneficiaries in any one village to form a co-operative society among themselves. The co-operative was to replace the former landowner in the organisation of cultivation, provision of credit and other inputs, and the marketing of produce. With the government concentrating its services through co-operatives, the system was extended beyond the boundaries of agrarian reform areas until it covered almost all of rural Egypt by the mid-1960s.

The organisation of supervised co-operatives was thus a systematic attempt by the State to control the functioning of the agricultural economy. In this sense it can be seen as the manifestation of the general drive towards State control and planning in the Egyptian economy and an extension of the bureaucratic apparatus to the rural areas. There were three basic instruments of control in the system. First, there was control through the agricultural engineer attached as a supervisor to the elected co-operative council. His writ extended to the enforcement of crop-rotation schedules, water control and the organisation of key farming operations such as mechanised ploughing, crop fumigation and pest control. Secondly, the co-operatives had a monopoly over the supply of key inputs such as chemical fertilisers, insecticides, seeds and institutionally provided credit. Thirdly, the co-operatives exercised control over the marketing of the most important crops and were also the instrument for enforcing the direct procurement of agricultural produce.

Having outlined the main features of the post-reform agrarian system, we shall now draw on available data to assess the effect of agrarian reform on rural Egypt. Here, we shall concentrate on the performance of the system in two areas: output growth and income distribution and poverty.

(i) Growth Performance

One of the interesting features of Egypt's co-operative system was the attempt to increase agricultural production through the introduction of the system of land and crop consolidation – thus reversing the effects of rapid fragmentation – and through the supply of improved inputs – seeds, fertilisers, pesticides, technical advice and, above all, credit. Available data suggest, however, that the period 1952-77, taken as a whole, was one of slow growth for Egyptian agriculture. The value of four of the major crops – cotton, wheat, maize and rice – increased from £E182 million in 1950 to £E232 million in 1975 (at constant 1950 prices), an average annual rate of growth of 1.2 per cent. But the growth of output was not even over this period. We can in fact distinguish between two major sub-periods in terms of growth performance. Table

Table 2.1:   Growth Performance of Egyptian Agriculture

	1960	1965	1969	1970	1971	1972	1973	1974
Value of output (£E)[a]	559	797	966	1 040	1 123	1 223	1 392	
Costs of inputs (£E)[a]	147	190	241	262	306	318	373	
Value added (£E)[a]	412	606	725	778	817	905	1 019	
Index of total output[b]	84	107	123	123	127	129	130	132
Index of output per capita[b]	88	102	105	102	102	101	99	97

	1956/61	1961/6	1966/71	1972/7
Average annual growth rates (percentage)[c]	3.5	4.0	2.0	2.0

Notes: a. At current prices.
b. FAO index (1961-5 =100) based on a weighted average of physical crop production.
c. Based on value added at constant prices.
Source: Central Agency for Public Mobilisation and Statistics (CAPMS), *Estimates of National Income from the Agricultural Sector*, various issues, and FAO, *Production Yearbook*, various issues.

2.1 shows that the average annual rate of growth of value added in agriculture at constant prices amounted to some 4 per cent during the 1950s and mid-1960s, then declined to 2 per cent between the mid-1960s and the 1970s. The improved performance during the first period must reflect, at least partially, the impact of improved co-operative services and the effect of the new rotation system. This is confirmed by the observed increase in productivity – as measured in terms of yields of major crops – during the same period. In 1965, indices of yields per feddan for the seven major crops (average 1948-51 = 100) amounted to: cotton 124; wheat 143; maize 167; millet 142; barley 137; rice 132; and sugar cane 130.[11] This initial improvement did not continue during the second period. The decade 1965-75 witnessed a negligible increase in the yields of these crops. Taking 1965 as a base, the yield indices in 1975 were: cotton 105; wheat 122; maize 102; millet 102; barley 111; rice 101; and sugar cane even declined to 92. This reflects the combined effects of a number of factors, most important of which were the increased waterlogging and salinity, the lack of continued investment in agricultural infrastructure and the fact that Egyptian agriculture has reached a stage where any increase in productivity was almost impossible given the techniques of production used. There is no doubt that Egyptian crop yields are high compared with world averages,[12] but not unduly so considering the country's warm climate and the fact that agriculture is fully irrigated. Had the co-operatives continued the initial push by introducing high-yield varieties and improved production techniques, and had the government carried out the planned investment in covered drainage, the impressive performance of the 1950s and 1960s could have continued.

A more disturbing aspect of the performance of Egyptian agriculture over the period studied is the decline in output per capita. Table 2.1 shows that after a modest increase in the index of output per capita during the 1960s, a slow but steady decline began by the early 1970s. This reflects the effect of a slow rate of growth of total output (2 per cent per year) combined with a rate of population growth of 2.5 per cent per annum. The deterioration in the land/man ratio, which began as early as the 1930s, had reached its critical limit by the 1970s. Neither the marginal additions to the arable land as a result of the High Dam nor the modest increase in productivity was sufficient to counterbalance the effects of this increase in rural population. These developments have serious implications not only for the future growth of agriculture, but also for the economy as a whole. With agriculture being unable to support the increase in population, rural-urban migration has been increasing at unprecedented rates. The 1976 Population Census reported that the proportion of urban to total population in Egypt was 44 per cent compared to 40.5 per cent in 1966 and 37.4 per cent in 1960.[13] Moreover, Egypt's agriculture is becoming less and less capable of supplying the growing population with its food needs, with a consequent increase in the country's dependence on imports and rapid inflation in food prices. Agricultural imports, which accounted for 34 per cent of total imports in the mid-1960s, have increased to 60 per cent since 1974.[14] Moreover, the government's desire to protect the population, especially the urban population, against increased food prices has led to the creation of a growing food subsidy programme which has had far-reaching effects on both imports and domestic production.[15] Wheat and flour alone account for about half of these imports. Moreover, the official wholesale price index of foodstuffs and beverages has almost doubled during the same period.[16]

(ii)   Income Distribution and Poverty

We have seen in the previous section that aggregate figures on production and yields show a moderate upward trend. The same has not, however, been true of the trend in average income per household in rural areas over this period. The picture that is revealed by the three surveys of household income and expenditure that are available is one of stagnation in real incomes between 1958/9 and 1974/5 where gains

Table 2.2:   Rural Household Expenditure

	Average Expenditure per Rural Household	Rural Consumer Price Index	Real Expenditure per Household
1958/9	£E147.7	100	£E147
1964/5	£E224.2	143	£E157
1974/5	£E375.5	237	£E158

Note: It should be noted that there are statistical objections to the procedure of inferring a trend from scattered observations from sample surveys, but there are some factors which tend to weaken the strength of these objections in the Egyptian case. The three surveys were all carried out by the same statistical agency (CAPMS) and form part of a regular national programme of sample surveys. This ensures consistency in definitions, concepts, sampling size and procedures, etc., which removes many of the objections to the making of intertemporal comparisons on the basis of these data. Moreover, all three surveys showed such consistency in the average household size of the sample that objections about the distorting effect of changes in demographic structure cannot be seriously entertained.
Source: CAPMS, *Family Budget Surveys*, 1958/9, 1964/5 and 1974/5.

in money incomes have been wiped away by a high rate of inflation (Table 2.2). These surveys are the official Family Budget Surveys carried out in 1958/9, 1964/5 and 1974/5. The figures on rural household expenditure from these surveys are as presented in Table 2.2.

It appears from Table 2.2 that while the average expenditure per household in money terms more than doubled between 1958/9 and 1974/5, there was only a slight increase in real terms during the period from 1958/9 to 1964/5 and a virtual stagnation in subsequent years.

Table 2.3: An Estimate of the Rural Poor in Egypt, 1958/9, 1964/5 and 1974/5

	1958/9	1964/5	1974/5
Household income corresponding to poverty line (£E)	93	125	270
Total population (000)	25 832	30 139	36 417
Rural population (000)	15 968	17 754	20 830
No. of rural families (000)	3 224	3 345	4 166
Families below poverty line:			
% of rural families	35.0	26.8	44.0
No.	1 160 640	903 150	1 833 000
Population below poverty line:			
% of rural population	22.5	17.0	28.0
No.	3 592 800	3 018 180	5 832 400

Source: For details on the data and methods used see S. Radwan, *Agrarian reform and rural development: Egypt 1952-1975* (Geneva, ILO, 1977), pp. 40-50.

It is clear, therefore, that the agrarian reform has not arrested the process of impoverishment in rural Egypt. It is of course possible that in the absence of agrarian reform this process might have occurred faster or with greater intensity. Indeed, the evidence of the temporary improvements in distribution up till the mid-1960s would be consistent with such an interpretation. Regardless of its temporary impact, it remains true that the reform did not change the system and that the fundamental forces which perpetuate poverty in rural Egypt have continued to operate. The outcome that we have observed in terms of increasing poverty is, to us, evidence of the ease with which these forces reassert themselves after a partial agrarian reform. These forces can be basically classified as those arising from diminishing access to land and the process of growing differentiation resulting from the operation of market forces leading to inflationary pressures. In addition, the inability of the industrial sector to provide employment opportunities for the growing rural labour force made it difficult to take the pressure off a stagnant agricultural sector. These pressures would have been reduced had the rate of industrial expansion been higher (as was the case in the Republic of Korea and Japan). The industrialisation drive of the 1960s has no doubt increased the contribution of industry to GDP growth. Industry contributed 25 per cent of the increase in real GDP between 1952/3 and 1959/60, and this contribution increased to 27 per cent between 1959/60 and 1969/70. Nevertheless, hopes that industrialisation will solve the country's employment problem caused by the inability of a land-scarce and labour-intensive agriculture to absorb the new entrants to the labour force are not yet fulfilled. Manufacturing created new jobs for 18 per cent of the increase in labour force between 1937 and 1960; and, despite the employment drive, for only 16 per cent of the increase between 1960 and 1970.[17]

In the post-agrarian reform period the rate of increase in the rural population has remained at almost 2.5 per cent per annum in spite of a rapid increase in urbanisation.[18] Between 1960 and 1970, the total rural population increased by 19 per cent, whereas the number of landholdings, an indicator of access to land, increased by only 12 per cent over a similar period (1961 to 1972).[19] This implies growing landlessness and a recent estimate shows that the proportion of landless families had increased from 40 to 45 per cent of those engaged in agriculture between 1961 and 1972.[20] Thus, apart from the once-and-for-all gain in terms of improved access to land (the extent of which we believe to be less than that given in previous estimates), the process of growing landlessness has continued. Continued growth in rural population and a highly unequal distribution of land ownership ensured this outcome.

It was not only limited access to land and continued inequality in land distribution that conditioned the neutralisation of the gains from the agrarian reform. A related process was the lack of countervailing power to protect real incomes, let alone increase them, in the face of rapid inflation in the 1960s and 1970s.

The Agrarian Question in the 1970s

An important question which emerges from the foregoing survey of Egypt's agrarian system is the extent to which there has been a change in the essentials of the 'agrarian question' over the last quarter of a century. As pointed out earlier, the 'agrarian question' before 1952 centred on an extremely unequal distribution of land ownership and a defective land tenure system. Successive land reforms attempted to 'solve' this question through a 'package' of reforms, including land redistribution, tenancy reform, minimum wage legislation and the establishment of co-operatives. This resulted in some initial gains in asset and income distribution and a reduction in rural poverty, but these were once-and-for-all gains which were eroded away as the system reverted to a new inegalitarian equilibrium. By the 1970s, the fundamental characteristics of the agrarian system remained unchanged: a system of private land ownership characterised by unequal distribution of land and income, widespread landlessness and an increase in the incidence of rural poverty.

It is extremely important to analyse first the main features of the new equilibrium, and secondly the major causes that explain the perpetuation of the essential characteristics of the system. Neither the available data nor the interpretations of various writers on the Egyptian economy provide sufficient answers to these questions.

A crucial question that occupies most writers is that of finding an appropriate framework for understanding these changes in the agrarian system: their extent and their limitations. Various writers have offered different interpretations. Anouar Abdel Malek, for instance, argues with Wittfogel that the key to the analysis of these changes is the central role of the State which has, for long, controlled the irrigation system, and, therefore, agriculture.[21] For M. Abdel Fadil agrarian reform can be seen as having paved the way for the virtual transition of Egypt's agrarian system from semi-feudalism into capitalism by eliminating the power of the very large landowners, and as a result of organising the labour market.[22] In contrast, Robert Mabro stresses the growing pressures on the agricultural sector arising from the unfavourable imbalance between land and people,[23] while Bent Hansen concentrates on the absence of allocative efficiency.[24] There is no doubt that each of these writers has pointed to an important element of the process of agrarian change. But none answers fully our question: how is it that such a significant agrarian reform has failed to alter the agrarian system in a fundamental way?

Any attempt to answer such a question in the absence of data would have been futile. A sample survey of rural households was therefore necessary first to update the existing data, and secondly to generate the new data needed to establish inter-relationships between various household characteristics and to test some hypotheses on the process of poverty generation.

Figure 2.1: Villages Chosen for the Survey

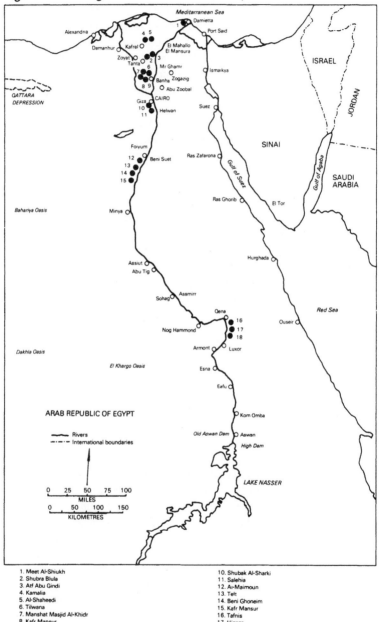

1. Meet Al-Shiukh
2. Shubra Blula
3. Atf Abu Gindi
4. Kamalia
5. Al-Shaheedi
6. Tilwana
7. Manshat Masjid Al-Khidr
8. Kafr Mansur
9. Manshat Abu Zikri

10. Shubak Al-Sharki
11. Salehia
12. Al-Maimoun
13. Telt
14. Beni Ghoneim
15. Kafr Mansur
16. Tafnis
17. Higaza
18. Al-Amiria

Methodology

The present study is almost entirely based on the results of a sample survey of rural households that we carried out in early 1977. In this section we shall briefly outline the main features of the survey, leaving technical details to the Appendix.

The Sample

A random sample of 1,000 households in 18 villages was drawn using the 1966 and 1976 Population Censuses as a frame. The sample size was partly dictated by considerations of comparability with the country's Household Budget Surveys, which usually cover the same number of households in each of their four rounds. The sample was selected through a multi-stage sampling procedure carried out as follows:[25]

First, the country was divided into strata according to the Governorate (administrative region) boundaries. Seven of the 25 Governorates were excluded because of their atypical features (being exclusively urban such as Cairo and Alexandria, or desert such as Sinai). From the list of the remaining 18 Governorates a random sample of 3 was chosen from each of the two major agro-ecological zones, *Upper* and *Lower* Egypt. These were: Damietta, Gharbia, Menufia, Giza, Beni Suef and Qena (see Figure 2.1).

Secondly, the total number of households in the sample was distributed among the six Governorates in proportion to their share of the total rural population of those Governorates.

Thirdly, a sample of 18 villages was chosen in such a way as to allow large and small villages to be represented in proportion to their respective shares in the six Governorates combined. A population of 5,000 in the 1966 Census was taken as the dividing line. According to this criterion, one-third of the villages were large and two-thirds small in 1966. Thus, six large and twelve small villages were drawn at random from the six Governorates according to these Governorates' shares of large and small villages.

Finally, the number of households to be drawn from each village was obtained by distributing the number of households to be drawn from each Governorate among the selected villages of the Governorate according to the relative population of these villages. Of the 1,000 households, 586 were to be drawn from the six large villages and 414 from the twelve small villages. A random sample corresponding to these numbers was drawn using the lists of the 1976 Population and

Housing Census as a frame.[26] Table 2.4 provides a summary of the sample distribution.

Table 2.4:   Distribution of the Household Sample by Governorate and Village

Governorate and Village	Markaz (District)	Total Population 1976	Total No. of Households 1976	No. of Households Selected
Damietta				
Meet Al-Shiukh	Farskour	2 794	560	56
Gharbia				
Shubra Blula El-Sakhawia	Kutour	5 378[a]	1 045	89
Atf Abu Gindi		1 429	321	24
Kamalia	Mahalla El-Kubra	2 460	386	36
Al-Shaheedi		4 644	178	77
Menufia				
Tilwana	Al-Bagour	6 121[a]	1 285	111
Manshat Masjid Al-Khidr		1 112	220	18
Kafr Mansur	Ashmoun	3 285	631	46
Manshat Abu Zikri	Quesna	4 047	697	36
Giza				
Shubak Al-Sharki	Al-Saff	13 176[a]	2 236	151
Salehia		1 793	386	23
Beni Suef				
Al-Maimoun	Al-Wasta	9 321[a]	2 080	62
Telt	Al-Fashn	5 141	1 063	33
Beni Ghoneim	Al-Wasta	1 722	375	11
Kafr Mansur	Beba	3 062	671	19
Qena				
Tafnis	Esna	6 921[a]	1 219	44
Higaza	Kous	17 959[a]	3 327	129
Al-Amiria	Abu Tesht	5 021	1 124	33

Note: a. Large villages.

The sample's representativeness of the rural society at large will be examined later by comparing the survey results to national data whenever available. A few observations may, however, be made at this stage. The geographical spread of the 18 villages in the sample was such that it ranged from the tip of the Delta (Meet Al-Shiukh – Damietta) to the south of the Nile Valley (Tafnis – Qena). Moreover, the villages represented a wide variety of rural economies with those which are purely agricultural (Tiwana-Menufia), those that can be considered extensions to urban centres (Shubak Al-Sharki – Giza), those with traditional handicrafts (head-cover making in Atf Abu Gindi – Gharbia), and those near a large industrial centre (Kamalia – Gharbia). Finally, some of the main characteristics of the household sample, such as the age and sex structure, employment patterns and income per head were not significantly different from the national data. In one aspect the sample was different from rural Egypt: the distribution of land-holding. A comparison of the survey results with the latest (1976) statistics on landholding shows that the sample may have failed to capture the upper end of the distribution. The analysis of the survey results should therefore be interepreted with this bias in mind.

Questionnaire Design

The questionnaires were specially designed for the survey, one to be administered at the household level and the other to collect data at the village level. The household survey represents a distinct departure from traditional Family Budget Surveys. The questionnaire was designed to generate data on the major correlates of rural poverty: distribution of land and other productive assets and changes therein, employment characteristics, levels of wages and their seasonal variations, consumption and access to basic needs and the use of co-operative services. The main purpose of the questionnaire was to generate data that are relevant to the conceptualisation of poverty in a rural economy. Thus the first task was to generate information which would help in the identification of the poor not only by constructing nutrition-based poverty lines, but also by drawing distributional profiles of the rural population from which we could associate various attributes of poverty with a key variable of the poor household such as income or type of employment. Secondly, the questionnaire aimed at providing data that could explain the shortfall in basic needs of the poor. This required posing questions on the access of households to productive assets, the extent of employment and unemployment and average earnings from labour (whether wage-employment or self-employment). Moreover, the questionnaire was designed in such a way as to generate data which would help in establishing inter-relationships between various household characteristics, such as the level of income and nutritional status, the employment pattern and ownership of assets and so on. Finally, an attempt was made to avoid posing direct questions concerning the income of the household. Alternatively, a number of questions sought to elicit information on income from various sources such as employment, agricultural production, non-agricultural activites and ownership of assets.

In view of these considerations the household survey included six 'modules':

(i)   household characteristics, providing the usual questions on the structure of the household;

(ii) employment, aiming at generating data on the occupational structure of the household, income from employment and seasonal fluctuations of both employment and income;

(iii) economic resources of the household covering ownership of assets, notably land and change over time in access to land, tenurial arrangements and the conditions under which they are contracted;

(iv) an income-production account eliciting data on agricultural production and income generated therefrom;

(v)   consumption, including a list of household consumption over the month preceding enumeration for food and the preceding year for other items of expenditure; and

(vi) access to co-operative services.

The village survey was designed to generate data at the local level, i.e. the village. Emphasis was laid on data concerning the provision of services, especially co-operative services, and the collection of data on prices and wages prevailing in the villages.

The results of the survey demonstrate the advantages of the approach outlined above. But a number of limitations should be emphasised at this point. First, the questions on employment were limited to the usual questions on length of employment in the primary and secondary occupation. No attempt was made to collect data on time use by the working members of the household. Thus it was difficult to reach accurate estimates on work intensity and underemployment. Secondly, the local-level survey did not include questions on many important aspects of village life, especially participation and the economic base of village society. It was hoped that the survey would be complemented by 'village profiles' based on direct interviewing of the villagers, but we were able to do this for one village only (see Appendix to Chapter 5). Finally, it should be borne in mind that the survey was applied only for one round and therefore the data may have failed to capture seasonal fluctuations. An attempt was made to ask questions about seasonal differences in employment and agricultural production, but the same was not done in the case of consumption.

Appendix: Sampling Procedure, Concepts and Definitions

Sampling Procedure

As mentioned in the text, a random sample of 1,000 households in 18 villages belonging to six Governorates was drawn through a multi-sampling procedure as shown below.

(a) The Governorate sample. Six Governorates were randomly selected, three in each of the two major ecological zones, Upper and Lower Egypt. The total number of households in the sample was distributed among the six Governorates in proportion to their share of the total rural population in those Governorates.[27] The rural population in the six Governorates according to the 1966 Population Census is shown in column 1 of Table A2.1. Column 2 shows the percentage share of each Governorate in the total rural population of the six. The number of households to be selected from each is shown in column 3.

Table A2.1: Total Population and Households in Sample Governorates

Name of Governorate	Rural Population (millions)	Share of Rural Population in the Sample (%)	No. of Households in the Sample[a]
Damietta	0.32	5.6	56
Gharbia	1.30	22.6	226
Menufia	1.22	21.2	213
Giza	1.00	17.4	174
Beni Suef	0.72	12.5	125
Qena	1.19	20.7	206
Total	5.75	100.0	1 000

Note: a. The number of households with valid answers may vary from time to time since 132 questionnaires were totally discarded and another 2 were not usable for some entries.

(b) The sample of villages. A stratified sample of 18 villages was selected where large and small villages were represented in their proportion in aggregate in the six Governorates. A population of 5,000 in 1966 was taken as the dividing line.[28] In the six Governorates a third of the villages were large in 1966 according to this criterion. Thus we

must have six large and twelve small villages in our sample of 18 to be drawn from six Governorates. The next step was to distribute these villages among the six Governorates according to their shares of large and small villages. The principle chosen was the following: if Governorate *i* had *x* per cent of the total number of large villages in the six Governorates then we select at random $(1/100) x$ (6) large villages from that Governorate. For small villages the formula, similarly, was $1/100\, x$ (12) where *x* was the percentage share of *i* in the total number of small villages in the six Governorates. Since whole villages (and not fractions) were to be chosen and since the total numbers chosen were small, the rounding error was large. According to the above criteria the numbers of large and small villages selected from each of the six Governorates were as follows.

Table A2.2:   Number of Villages in Sample by Size

Name of Governorate	No. of Large Villages	No. of Small Villages	Total No. of Villages
Damietta	0	1	1
Gharbia	1	3	4
Menufia	1	3	4
Giza	1	1	2
Beni Suef	1	3	4
Qena	2	1	3
Total	6	12	18

(c) The household sample. The selection of villages by random sampling, according to the schedule in Table A2.2, was made. These are listed in Table A2.3 with the number of households to be drawn from each shown against their names. These numbers have been arrived at as follows: from Table A2.1 we knew the number of households to be drawn from each Governorate. This was divided among the villages of the Governorates according to the relative population of these villages in 1966. To put it formally, from each selected village in Governorate *i j* a sample of r_{ij} households was randomly drawn according to the following formula:

Table A2.3: The Sample Frame

Name of Governorate	Selected Large Village(s)	Population in 1966	No. of Households to be Drawn from the Large Village	Selected Small Village(s)	Population in 1966	No. of Households to be Drawn from the Small Village
Damietta	—		—	Meet Al-Shiukh	2 118	56
Gharbia	Shubra Blula El-Sakhawia	5 020	89	Atf Abu Gindi Kamalia Al-Shaheedi	1 364 1 978 4 382	24 36 77
Menufia	Tilwana	6 334	111	Kafr Mansur Manshat Masjid Al-Khidr Manshat Abu Zikri	2 611 1 029 2 126	46 18 38
Giza	Shubak Al-Sharki	10 877	151	Salehia	1 656	23
Beni Suef	Al-Maimoun	8 909	62	Telt Beni Ghoneim Kafr Mansur (Markaz Beba)	4 793 1 528 2 624	33 11 19
Oena	Tafnis Higaza	6 216 18 344	44 129	Al-Amiria	4 703	33
Total			586			414

$$r_{ij} = \frac{P_{ij}}{\displaystyle\sum_{j=1}^{N_i} P_{ij}} \ S_i \ (i = 1, ...,6)$$

where: S_i = number of sample households in Governorate i
P_{ij} = population of village j in Governorate i
N_i = number of sample villages in Governorate i

(d) The sample frame. The 1966 Population Census was used as a frame for the selection of the Governorate and the village samples, as the preliminary results of the 1976 Census became available only on the eve of the survey and in a summary form. Thus, the 1976 Census results were used as a frame for the household sample since it was the most accurate and up-to-date list of the population available. To ensure consistency, a number of checks were carried out (such as relative sizes of Governorates, numbers of villages and average size of households within the villages of the sample). No serious inconsistencies were found.

Concepts and Definitions

A manual of *'Instructions to Enumerators'* was prepared to guide the interviewers through the questionnaire. The following extracts will concentrate on the definitions of some of the important variables and the concepts underlying the questions.

(a) The household. A household has been defined as:

An individual or group of individuals, whether relatives or not, who live permanently in the same accommodation (house, part of a house, a room or a hut), eat from the same kitchen (or pot), and depend on a joint budget usually controlled by the household head. *Guests* are not to be included except if they have been staying over the last six months. *Servants* are to be included if they share the household food and accommodation. An *absent member* of the family should be counted if his absence is temporary (at school, university, travelling, etc.).

A *household head* is defined as 'the person, male or female, who is regarded by household members as the head. He is usually responsible for the direction of the family's expenditure policy and has the highest income, but is not necessarily the oldest.'

(b) Employment. A distinction was made between *'main'* and *'secondary'* occupation. The main occupation is defined as the one in which the respondent usually spends most of his time. Where there is more than one 'secondary occupation', only the one in which, among the secondary occupations, he usually spends most time was entered.

'Days worked' for each season includes all days spent in agricultural work in connection with the crop of that season and which fall within the reference period, i.e. the twelve-month period preceding enumeration. Where work in connection with a crop was done more than twelve months before, it was excluded. Similarly, in connection with a standing crop the work done up until enumeration day was included. *'Agricultural work'* is defined as 'cultivating, harvesting and threshing' and nothing else.

A day is defined as a standard working day (i.e. what the respondent considers as a full working day).

'Wage rate' refers to the cash value of all daily wage payments received, whether in cash or in kind. The imputed value of payments in kind was arrived at by asking the respondents what cash value they placed on the payments in kind that they received. For military conscripts the value of board and lodging received was taken as £E270 per year and this sum was added to any cash payments received. For off-farm workers the 'total wage' refers to their total earnings during the year preceding enumeration.

'Total labour force' was defined as all members of the household between the ages of 12 and 65 (to be consistent with the Population Census definition). *'Civilian labour force'* was defined as total labour force *minus* regular army and conscripts of the national service. *'Agricultural labour force'* included only those whose occupation was 'farmer or family farm worker' and/or 'farm labourer'. A distinction was made between *casual* and *permanent* farm labourers where the former had no fixed employer and the latter worked for the same employer for most days of the year.

The degree of *'unemployment'* was measured as the shortfall of days worked from a full working year of 280 days. *'Underemployment'* was gauged by asking the question 'Do you think you could have worked more over the last year?' It is obvious that estimates based on answers of this attitudinal question should not be considered more than indicative and provide no substitute for time-use study.

(c) Ownership of assets. The household was the enumeration unit for all the questions concerning the ownership of assets.

The value of assets refers to the estimated current market value. This was obtained by asking the respondent to estimate the amount he would receive if he were to sell the asset today.

To estimate *land movements* questions were asked about the change (gain/loss) in the ownership of land over three periods: last year, last five years and over lifetime.

For other assets, the change over the last year was recorded to estimate *capital formation* and change in stock.

A *house* was defined as the living premises of the family, whether it was a separate house, flat, cottage, or hut.

(d) Farm production. The reference period for the questions on farm production was the agricultural year preceding the survey. Questions were related to seasons and crops separately.

The *'marketed surplus'* was estimated as the difference between total output and retained output *plus* rent paid in kind. *'Retained output'* refers to that part which is not sold, used as payment in kind of rent and wages (or used as an input into items that are sold, e.g. wheat retained to produce bread which is sold).

(e) Household income. *'Total household income'* was defined as the sum of income from all sources. These were: total wage earnings from work on other farms plus total wage-earnings from non-farm work in village plus total earnings from off-farm work outside village plus total net earnings from family plus income from rental of land and machinery plus income from non-agricultural productive assets plus remittances received.

'Income from family farm' was defined as the total value of agricultural output and complementary activities (dairy, poultry, etc.) over the last year after deducting the outlays incurred during the same period (rent of land, value of fodder, running costs of machinery, fertilisers and other inputs, wages for hired farm labour and taxes).

(f) Household expenditure. This relates to the current expenditure by the household. The reference period for food consumption was the previous month, and the previous year for other items (clothing, consumer durables, medical services, etc.).

The *unit of enumeration* was the household. However, a question was asked about the 'number of persons boarding in the household during the month preceding enumeration day' in order to establish the consumption unit to which the subsequent data refer. Normally, this unit should be identical to the household, but we had to allow for the possibility that household members may be temporarily absent and that there may be guests who stay for a prolonged period.

All calculations of *per capita* consumption, calorie intake and expenditure were made after converting all household members to *adult equivalent units* using the following scale:

adult male	(12-65 years)	1.0
adult female	(12-65 years)	1.0
aged	(65 years)	0.7
children	(0-12 years)	0.5

List of Village Prices[a]

Item	Unit	Price in piastres
Food, beverages and tobacco		
Wheat	kilah	71
Maize	kilah	65
Rice	kg	10
Beans	kadah	20
Lentils	kadah	32
Meat	kg	42
Fish (fresh)	kg	54
Eggs	dozen	39
Vegetable oil (non-ration)	kg	36
Ghee	lb	54
Potatoes	kg	10
Onions	kg	8
Tomatoes	kg	10
Oranges	kg	7
Dates	kg	14
Sugar (non-ration)	kg	33
Tea	ounce	15
Cigarettes	1 packet of 20	10
Tobacco	ounce	8
Soap	piece	3
Kerosene	tin	20
Clothing		
Raw cotton textiles *(Dammour)*	metre	7
Printed cotton *(Kastour)*	metre	15
Local woolen cloth *(Mahalla/Stea)*	metre	300
Footwear *(Bulgha/Markoub)*	pair	150

Note: a. Refers to those retail prices prevailing in the village at time of enumeration.

Notes

1. The intricate history of land ownership in Egypt has been the subject of several excellent studies. See in particular I. Amer: *Land and peasant: The agrarian question in Egypt* (Cairo, Dar El-Nahda, 1958); G. Baer: *A history of landownership in modern Egypt, 1800-1950* (London, Oxford University Press, 1962); Rauf Abbas Hamid: *The social system of Egypt under large landowners, 1837-1914* (Cairo, Dar El-Fikr Al Hadirh, 1973); and Asem A. El-Dessouky: *Large landowners and their role in Egyptian society, 1914-1952* (Cairo, Dar Al-Thakafa Al-Jadida, 1975).

2. 1 feddan = 1.038 acres = 0.42 hectare = 4.201 square metres.

3. E.Eshag and M. A. Kamal: 'Agrarian reform in the UAR (Egypt)' in *Bulletin of the Oxford University Institute of Economics and Statistics*, May 1968, pp. 77-8.

4. M. Abdel-Fadil: *Development, income distribution and social change in rural Egypt 1952-1970*, Occasional Paper No. 45 (University of Cambridge, Department of Applied Economics, 1975), p. 14.

5. Ibid., p. 15.

6. S. Radwan: *Agrarian reform and rural development: Egypt 1952-1975* (Geneva, ILO, (1977), p. 7.

7. The subject of land reform became most controversial during the 1940s. Various projects were discussed in the press or submitted to Parliament, notably the bill of Mr M. Khattab to limit the size of land ownership by 50 feddans, the call by Mureit Ghali (in his book *The agrarian reform*) to raise the ceiling to 100 feddans, and the argument by Sadek Saad (in his book *The problem of the fellah*) that the State should expropriate land above 50 feddans and run it as collectives. For interesting details see Abdel-Azim Ramadan: 'The revolution and agrarian reform', in *Al-Kateb* (Cairo), August 1971.

8. Radwan, *Agrarian reform and rural development*, p. 29.

9. Ibid., p. 23.

10. See K. B. Griffin: *The political economy of agrarian change* (London, Macmillan, 1973) for a full statement of these arguments.

11. Robert Mabro: *The Egyptian economy, 1952-1972* (Oxford, Clarendon Press, 1974), p. 81.

12. World Bank, *Egyptian agriculture development problems, constraints and alternatives* (Washington, DC, 1976), p. 13.

13. CAPMS: *1976 Population Census: Preliminary results* (Cairo, 1977), p. 9.

14. United Nations: *Yearbook of international trade statistics*, various issues.

15. For detailed studies on Egypt's food system and the role of subsidies see W. Cuddihy: *Agricultural price management in Egypt*, World Bank Staff Working Paper No. 388 (Washington, DC, 1980);, and United States Department of Agriculture: *Strategies for accelerating agricultural development* (Washington, DC, 1982).

16. CAPMS: *Monthly Bulletin of Consumer Price Indices*, various issues. The index amounted to 190.3 per cent in 1975 with base year 1965/6 = 100.

17. For details see R. Mabro and S. Radwan: *The industrialisation of Egypt: 1939-1973* (Oxford, Clarendon Press, 1976).

18. Abdel-Fadil, *Development, income distribution and social change*, Ch. 6.

19. Radwan, *Agrarian reform and rural development*, Table 2.3.

20. Ibid.

21. A. Abdel Malek: *Egypt: Military society* (New York, Vintage Books, Random House, 1968), pp. 353ff.

22. Abdel-Fadil, *Development, income distribution and social change*.

23. Mabro, *The Egyptian Economy*.

24. B. Hansen and K. Nashashibi: *Foreign trade regimes and economic development: Egypt* (New York, Columbia University Press, 1975).

25. For details see the Appendix to Chapter 2.

26. The 1966 Population Census was used as a frame in drawing the Governorate and village samples and. as the 1976 Population and Housing Census became available just on the eve of the survey. it was used to draw the household sample. Since the household sample was drawn from a frame different from that of the Governorate and village samples. a number of checks were performed to ensure consistency. No serious inconsistencies were found.

27. The definition of 'rural' used here is that of the Population Census. where the breakdown between rural and urban is based on administrative distinction: the urban population includes all people counted in the major urban Governorates. capitals of all other Governorates and capitals of 'Markaz' (district).

28. The cut-off point of 5.000 inhabitants in distinguishing between small and large villages is the criterion used by the Egyptian Family Budget Surveys.

3   The Generation and Distribution of Income

In the previous chapters we outlined the dimensions and principal manifestations of rural poverty and the economic framework which generated this poverty. That economic framework was defined by the power structure, and the role of the State in determining the nature and terms of economic relationships within the rural economy as well as the crucial role of the distribution of the ownership of productive assets in determining the structure of incomes and poverty. In this chapter we attempt a more detailed analysis of the process of income generation and its distribution.

Sources of Income

Description

A useful starting point would be to analyse the sources of income in our sample households in terms of factor shares (Table 3.1). It is

Table 3.1:   Distribution of Total Income by Source

	Income (£E)	%
Wages: other farms[a]	40 846	12.3
Wages: off-farm in village[b]	30 882	9.3
Wages: outside village[c]	81 264	24.5
Family farm with labour input	114 115	34.4
Family farm without labour input	6 001	1.8
Rent from land	4 535	1.4
Rent: equipment and livestock	3 334	1.0
Non-agricultural productive assets	33 305	10.0
Remittances	17 402	5.2
Total	331 684	100.0

Notes: a. Refers throughout this study to wage-earnings by household members from employment on farms other than that of the family.
b. Refers throughout this study to wages received by household members from non-farm employment within the village.
c. Refers throughout this study to wages received by household members from any type of employment outside the village.

immediately striking that for an extremely land-scarce agrarian society, the share of rent in total income (i.e. total *household* income) is only 1.4 per cent and that even allowing for other forms of property income (non-agricultural productive assets, rent of equipment and livestock) the share of this non-labour income amounts to only 12.4 per cent. At the same time the share of pure labour income is high for what appears to be a predominantly peasant-based agrarian society; 46 per cent of total income comes from wages (both on-farm and off-farm). The share of income emanating from family farms, a mixed category from the point of view of factor income, accounts for the remainder. We are thus left with a complex picture which contrasts sharply with descriptions of the process of income generation in rural economies as the simple binary opposition of landlords and tenant farmers or of some distributive permutation between landlords, tenants and proletarianised erstwhile peasants.

This complexity can be seen if we separate income derived directly from agricultural activity and that which is not. By this classification, we find that only 50 per cent of total income is derived from agriculture (36 per cent from family farms, 12 per cent from agricultural wages and 2.4 per cent from rent of land and other agricultural assets). One-third of total income comes from off-farm wages and off-farm wages outside the village are particularly important, accounting for almost one-quarter of the total income. Income from non-agricultural enterprises and assets accounts for another 10 per cent of total income and remittances for the remaining 5 per cent. We thus have a situation where, in a poor rural economy, agricultural activity generates only one-half of the total income.

The compexity lies not only in the diversity of income sources at the aggregate level but also in the fact that the diversity of income sources is characteristic of most households. This emerges from the data in Table 3.2 showing the distribution of household 'income claims' by source of income. A household is defined as having an 'income claim' from a particular source where such income features in the total income of that household. The table shows that, on the average, each household has two 'income claims' or sources of income. In column three of the table we show the percentages of the total number of households in our sample which have an income claim from each of the nine sources of income. It emerges that 48 per cent of households receive income from the 'family farms' involving the cultivation of land[1] and that 35 per cent receive income from agricultural wages. Particularly striking is the fact that very high percentages of total households receive income from sources external to the village; 30 per cent of all households have wage-earnings from outside the village and 23 per cent receive remittances. Thus extra-village sources of income do not only account for 30 per cent of total income that is received in the rural economy but also affect the total household earnings of a similar proportion of the total number of households. It is also striking that as many households receive income from off-farm wage-employment as from a family farm – 48 per cent of all households in each case.

Table 3.2:   Distribution of Household 'Income Claims' by Source

	No. of Income Claims	% Distribution of Claims	% of All Households Having an Income Claim from Each Source
Wages: other farms	305	17.9	35.2
Wages: off-farm in village	163	9.6	18.8
Wages: outside village	261	15.3	30.1
Family farm with labour input	418	24.5	48.2
Family farm without labour input	185	10.8	21.3
Rent from land	54	3.2	6.2
Rent: equipment and livestock	21	1.2	2.4
Non-agricultural productive assets	98	5.7	11.3
Remittances	201	11.8	23.2
Total	1 706	100.0	(Non-additive)

Notes: The figures refer to total income of households over the calendar year preceding the survey. 'Family farm with labour input' refers to earnings from family operated farms where at least one member of the household is engaged in farming operations on the farm. The category 'family farm without labour input' refers to cases where the household members only manage the farm and do not supply labour for farming operations. 'Rent of land' includes the imputed value of payments in kind under share-cropping arrangments and is gross of land taxes.

The low share of total income derived from rent of land merits some elaboration. Although 6 per cent of all households have rent as a source of income, only 1.4 per cent of total income is accounted for by rent. This is probably accounted for by the fact that the average area rented out per household is relatively small (see Table 4.11 in the next chapter).

The basic explanation for the fact that rent features marginally in total income lies in the fact that less than 50 per cent of households have agriculture as their main source of income and that of these a high proportion are households headed by landless agricultural labourers. Furthermore, the size of the rental market in land is relatively small – only 18 per cent of landowning households rent out land and such households comprise only 6 per cent of all households in our sample. The average level of rent is also low in relation to land values and farming incomes. The average value of rent paid was £E1.56 per kirat ($1/24$ of a feddan) being 2.7 per cent of the average value of land £E58.8 per kirat. In addition, the average total value of rent paid was £E53, compared with an average total income of £E334 for households headed by pure tenants. This moderate significance of the rental market and low levels of rent are probably explained by the existence of rent control.[2] A ceiling on rents reduces the attractiveness of renting out and also explains an observed level of rent that is well below that expected in an extremely land-scarce economy.

It should be noted, however, that these observations are subject to qualifications about the interpretation of data on tenancy relationships that we discuss in Chapter 4.

The structure of employment also bears out the importance of non-agricultural sources of livelihood (Table 3.3). Of the total labour force only 60 per cent were directly employed in agriculture as their main occupation (44 per cent on family farms and 16 per cent wage employees on 'other farms'). Another 18 per cent were in government employment (civilian and military) with a further 16 per cent in crafts, industry and service occupations.

Table 3.3:   Employment Structure

Main Occupation	No. of Workers	%
Farmer	647	43.7
Farm labourer	236	15.9
Craftsman or industry	120	8.1
Construction and service worker	116	7.8
Government employment	148	10.0
Military	113	7.6
Others	70	4.7
Looking for work	30	2.0
Total	1 480	100.0

Note: 'Looking for work' refers to those household members between the ages of 12 and 65 who were actively looking for work but did not work at all during the year preceding the date of enumeration.

The fact that agricultural employment is a larger proportion of total employment than agricultural income is of total income testifies to the generally higher average incomes to be derived from 'non-agricultural productive assets' followed closely by wage-earnings from outside the village (Table 3.4). In contrast, wage-employment on other farms yields an average value of less than half of that obtained from wage-earnings outside the village and is also 30 per cent lower than incomes from non-farm wage-employment within the village.

Table 3.4 Average Value of Each 'Income Claim' by Source of Income

	£E	Ranking
Wages: other farms	134	6
Wages: off-farm in village	188	4
Wages: outside village	311	2
Family farm with labour input	273	3
Family farm without labour input	32	9
Rent from land	84	8
Rent: equipment and livestock	159	5
Non-agricultural productive assets	340	1
Remittances	87	7

Table 3.5 Average Daily Earnings by Activity

	£E per Day
Work on family farm	0.9805
Wage-employment on other farms	0.5680
Off-farm wage-employment in village	0.7760
Off-farm wage-employment outside village	1.0000

Note: Figures refer to total earnings from each source of income divided by the total number of days worked in that activity. Thus the figure for 'work on family farm' is not strictly comparable with the others because it includes returns to land and other factors of production.

The same point also emerges in a comparison of the average daily earnings for the four sources of income with a clearly identifiable labour input (Table 3.5). The highest earnings are from wage-employment outside the village (an average of £E1 per day), while wage-employment on other farms yields only £E0.568. Off-farm employment within the village yields a return in between these two values while the returns from working on the family farm are marginally lower than those from wage-employment outside the village.

Interpretation

The basic fact that needs to be explained is the startlingly high proportion of our sample households that is engaged in non-agricultural activities: 50 per cent when classified by the main occupation of all individuals who are in the labour force. Although these proportions are higher than those revealed by earlier estimates, it should be noted that they were already high then and the trend had been upward. For example, Mabro estimates, on the basis of the 1969/70 Census figures, that only 67 per cent of employment in the 'provinces' was agricultural while 'services' accounted for 25 per cent. Moreover, 'nearly half of all new jobs in the provinces were created in the tertiary sector'.[3]

Two inter-related characteristics of Egypt provide the essential explanation. The first is the blurred distinction between town and country in the Egyptian context. 'The rural habitat is not dispersed, with isolated houses in the fields, but concentrated in small, densely populated settlements.'[4] Large villages (up to a population of 5,000) in this context would thus have many urban attributes and would be considered towns in other countries. Furthermore, the 'countryside' of Egypt is, for the most part, a thin ribbon of land on either bank of the Nile. Settlements are thus linear and 'market towns almost equidistant from each other (30-40 km) form a long string along the valley and a tight network in the Delta'.[5] The physical and economic distance between village and town is thus very small and the 'commuting rural-urban migrant' can exist as an economic category.

Given these spatial parameters, it has become possible for some of the adaptation to population pressure on the very limited arable land to take place in the countryside itself. Whereas in most countries mounting population pressure and/or growing differentials in income and economic opportunity between town and country have been reflected in an exodus from the countryside, in Egypt this has not necessarily been so. Scope has also existed for a transfer to a non-agricultural livelihood without a physical move out of the village. The high proportion of 'service' income (e.g. from petty production and trading) and the significant numbers of commuting government employees and industrial construction workers testify to this phenomenon.

It might be objected, however, that the high observed share of non-agricultural income might simply reflect biases in our sample where untypical pei-urban villages have had a disproportionate influence (Table 3.6). This objection does not appear to have much validity since a village-by-village breakdown of sources of income shows that the phenomenon is fairly generalised. Only two villages have a proportion of off-village income in total income of less than 10 per cent and half of the total number of villages have a value of within 10 percentage points of the mean value of 25 per cent. A re-classification by Governorate also reveals no extreme variations; the percentage of off-village income ranges from 16 to 35 per cent.

Table 3.6   Percentage of Total Income from Outside Village Sources

Village	Sample Households	% Total Income from Outside Village Source
Meet Al-Shiukh	54	35.3
Shubra Blula El-Sakhawia	86	16.0
Atf Abu Gindi	19	43.2
Kamalia	34	25.8
Al-Shaheedi	57	6.7
Tilwana	85	35.6
Manshat Masjid Al-Khidr	15	45.5
Kafr Mansur	36	15.5
Manshat Abu Zikri	28	16.5
Shubak Al-Sharki	142	34.7
Salehia	15	33.7
Al-Maimoun	59	11.0
Telt	10	25.0
Beni Ghoneim	33	27.7
Kafr Mansur	15	30.3
Tafnis	43	6.3
Higaza	103	22.5
Al-Amiria	33	23.3
Total/average	867	24.5

Source of Income by Income Group

After this examination of the sources of income in the aggregate, it will be useful to analyse the differences between income groups in terms of the composition of income. Such an analysis will provide a rough mapping of factor-share analysis to a size-distribution of income and will also provide an insight into the determinants of poverty and wealth in the Egyptian rural economy.

We have established in the previous section that the process of income generation does not correspond to a simple binary opposition of landlords and landless labourers or to some permutation of agrarian classes. This observation is reinforced by an analysis of income generation for different income groups. Particularly striking is the fact that we cannot have a clean delineation of income groups by source of income. There is, for instance, no clearly identifiable 'landlord class' at the top of the income scale nor a group of landless labourers making up the poor. There are systematic variations in income sources along the income scale but, while the 'weight' of different sources varies, the observation of the existence of a diversity of income sources holds true for all income groups. The only category with a large number of empty cells in the source-of-income matrix (Table 3.7) is that for income from the 'rent from equipment and livestock'. We cannot, therefore, use factor share as an unambiguous yardstick of differentiation in the rural economy since there is no clear mapping from factor income to the size-distribution of incomes.

Although there are no simple boundaries, systematic variations do exist and these variations do give a first approximation to some of the major correlates of rural poverty.

It is clearly noticeable that the bottom three income classes, in terms of average household income (constituting 10 per cent of the total number of households), have a very high concentration of single-member households (average household size for the bottom income class was 1.57) as well as a high proportion of disabled persons. The main source of income is 'remittances', which range from 76 per cent of total income for the poorest to 39 per cent for the third poorest income group. Moreover, 75 per cent of all households within these three income classes receive remittances. A corollary is that income from production and from rent is relatively insignificant; of the 80 households in these income classes only 18 receive wages from agricultural work and only 11 have farming income. Also significant is the fact that there is only one household with off-farm earnings from outside the village. Income from farming constitutes no more than about 10 per cent of total income while farm wages account only for 11 to 28 per cent of total income.

However, the share of income from agriculture increases sharply for the next two income classes; more than 30 per cent of total income is accounted for by agricultural wages while farming income accounts for more than 20 per cent. Indeed, these two income groups (accounting for 20 per cent of households) have the highest proportion of income coming from agricultural wages, indicating a high concentration of landless agricultural labourer households within this income range. Off-farm income, both from within and outside the village, also assumes greater significance, but the share of income from remittances falls sharply.

Table 3.7: Sources of Income

Income Class (£E)	No. of Households	Average Household Size	Wages: Other Farms		Wages: Off-farm in Village		Wages: Outside Village		Family Farm (with labour input only)	
			X	Y	X	Y	X	Y	X	Y
Less than 50.0	21	1.57	3	67	—	—	—	—	2	-52
50.0-74.9	25	2.08	4	45	4	22	—	—	4	41
75.0-99.9	34	2.12	11	48	7	57	1	61	5	46
100.0-149.9	71	4.23	34	98	16	79	3	75	21	88
150.0-199.9	96	4.46	46	113	16	126	14	150	38	118
200.0-249.9	96	4.89	42	133	15	139	27	172	38	128
250.0-299.9	93	5.75	38	131	19	180	24	216	42	179
300.0-349.9	68	6.22	25	138	10	203	22	264	40	206
350.0-399.9	64	5.80	21	106	10	199	26	296	33	245
400.0-499.9	97	6.75	33	190	25	272	38	291	51	244
500.0-599.9	60	7.92	21	205	10	322	32	287	41	322
600.0-799.9	70	8.20	13	203	18	254	35	396	49	396
800.0-999.9	32	9.63	9	126	9	231	21	516	22	363
1 000.0-1 399.9	21	10.48	2	71	4	190	12	553	17	616
1 400.0-1 999.9	14	12.21	3	234	1	144	5	876	12	1 099
2 000.0 and above	4	12.50	—	—	—	—	1	540	3	685
Averages	866	(5.93)	305	134	164	188	261	311	418	273
Total				40 846		30 882		81 267		114 115

Note: X = Number of households.   Y = Mean income from each source.

Table 3.7:   Sources of Income (contd)

	Rent from Land		Rent from Equipment and Livestock		Non-agricultural Productive Assets		Remittances		Average Income per House-hold from all Sources	Average Total Income per capita
	X	Y	X	Y	X	Y	X	Y		
Less than 50.0	—	—	—	—	—	—	18	30	34	21.66
50.0-74.9	3	14	—	—	—	—	18	48	63	30.29
75.0-99.9	1	61	—	—	4	65	23	51	89	41.98
100.0-149.9	3	23	—	—	7	109	25	45	128	30.26
150.0-199.9	4	70	—	—	8	138	22	71	178	39.91
200.0-249.9	6	101	—	—	11	179	16	62	228	46.63
250.0-299.9	4	66	1	3	12	212	8	139	275	47.83
300.0-349.9	4	19	3	38	6	193	10	96	325	52.25
350.0-399.9	2	60	1	10	10	270	6	87	376	64.83
400.0-499.9	7	90	—	—	12	293	17	102	443	65.63
500.0-599.9	1	15	1	3	5	318	10	52	543	68.56
600.0-799.9	8	136	3	57	11	422	10	195	682	83.17
800.0-999.9	5	147	1	30	6	670	8	83	876	90.97
1 000.0-1 399.9	3	123	6	221	2	640	5	293	1 113	106.20
1 400.0-1 999.9	2	61	4	320	2	1 030	2	330	1 631	133.58
2 000.0 and above	1	51	1	400	2	2 850	1	1 500	2 561	204.88
Averages		84		159		340		87		
Total	54	4 535	21	3 334	98	33 305	199	17 402		

As we move up the income scale the share of income from farming increases steadily, reaching a peak of 58 per cent of total income for the second-highest income class. At the same time, however, there is a parallel fall in the share of income coming from agricultural wages. The share of income from earnings derived from off-village employment also increases and accounts for no less than one-quarter of total income for income classes 8 to 14 (approximately the top 45 per cent of households).

Income from assets shows a mixed pattern. Rent from land remains a very low proportion of total income for all income classes and income from non-agricultural productive assets also shows no pronounced variations until the highest income class. Income from the rental of equipment and livestock features only in the upper income classes. Rental income does not constitute a substantial share of total income. The only exception is the topmost income class where 56 per cent of total income is accounted for by earnings from non-agricultural productive assets alone.

We can summarise these patterns as follows. There is in general a multiplicity of income sources for all income groups and no simple mapping from a functional to a size-distribution of income is possible. None the less, some broad patterns are discernible. The very poor, i.e. the bottom 10 per cent of households, have all the symptoms of chronic poverty: high dependence on transfer payments, a high proportion of disabled people (19 to 30 per cent of all individuals in these three income classes, whereas it does not exceed 3 per cent in any other income class), and a high proportion of single-member households headed by old persons. Above this hard-core poverty group, income levels are broadly related to the pattern of household economic activity. Families engaged predominantly in agricultural labour form the next 20 per cent of households, but beyond this group rising incomes are associated with access to land (reflecting the rising share of income from 'family farm') and access to off-village income-earning opportunities. Only at the very top of the income scale does rental income assume a dominant influence on income levels.

It is also worthy of notice that for most income groups income derived from 'non-agricultural productive assets' accounts for some 5 to 10 per cent of total income. From the qualitative descriptions in the completed questionnaires we know that this category refers to a variety of handicrafts, petty commodity production and trading activites. The significant presence of this category of income is thus in line with our hypothesis of impoverished adaptation by sections of the population who have no alternative source of livelihood. In this case, it would appear that a petty commodity production and service sector has grown up within the village and that this is of significant proportions if we include in this category not only the earnings from 'non-agricultural productive assets' but also part of the earnings from 'off-farm employment within the village'. (This accounts for between 5 to 15 per cent of total income for most income groups.) Evidence that such a process of labour re-allocation is taking place is also provided by the figures on the relative returns to labour input that were cited earlier. Earnings from work on 'family farms' are among the highest, but for a family that loses (or fails to gain) access to land there is the prospect of agricultural wage-employment at half the level of that enjoyed by 'landed' families. But the returns from agricultural wage-employment are in fact lower than those of off-farm employment in the village; there would thus have been a tendency for this sector to grow. This is even more true for wage-employment outside the village which offers a return higher than that even from the family farm. In addition, for those with access to capital the acquisition of non-agricultural productive assets offers the prospect of the highest return.

The above description is speculative but would appear more plausible if we remember that the rural economy is not a closed system but one with close links with the urban economy in terms of remittances and labour and commodity flows. Important income-generating activites in our sample are 'rural' in only a geographical but not economic sense, as evidenced by the importance of 'disguised migration' and a village-based commodity-production sector which primarily serves urban markets. It seems clear that a further stage of research will be required to chart the characteristics of this emerging 'parallel economy' phenomenon, the existence of which (on a substantial scale) was unexpected and had not been provided for in the research design.

The Size-distribution of Income

The average annual income per household derived from our survey was £E384, a figure which is closely comparable to the figure of £E375 shown by the 1974/5 Family Budget Survey. In view of the rise in the rural consumer price index between 1974/5 and 1977, our figures show a probable slight reduction in average real incomes between those two years. Indeed, piecing together information from our survey results and the three other household surveys on rural incomes stretching back to 1958/9, it appears that real incomes of rural households have largely stagnated.[6]

The average household income is extremely low: our estimate of the 'poverty line' for the period covered by our survey was £E395 for an average household of 5.9 members (see Chapter 5). The mean household income was thus *lower* than the poverty income level. At such a low level of average income, the degree of inequality in the distribution of income naturally assumes very acute significance. Even if incomes were distributed with perfect equality, the entire rural population would be just below poverty levels.

In the following sections, therefore, we shall estimate the degree of income inequality revealed by our survey data and this will serve as a general background for the detailed study of the incidence and intensity of poverty that will be presented in Chapter 5.

Overall Inequality

Taking the commonly used measure of inequality, the Gini coefficient for the size-distribution of total household income, we have a value of 0.3931. This figure is in the average range of inequality for the distribution of rural incomes in developing countries.[7]

It is also virtually identical with the value obtained from the 1974/5 survey of consumer expenditure for Egypt.[8] Apart from being an indication of the consistency of our results with those of other independent surveys, it also points to the absence of any significant shift in the overall distribution of rural incomes between 1975 and 1977.

As is well known, however, such a summary measure is of limited value where there are large variations in household size according to income class. This is indeed strikingly so in the case of Egypt. As Table 3.7 shows, household size rises steadily from 1.57 for the lowest income class to 12.5 for the highest. Therefore, the degree of inequality is significantly lower when an adjustment is made for this variation in family size. For example, using the grouped data to make this adjustment (i.e. dividing the average household income by the average household size for that income group), we find that the range in average income per household drops sharply from 75.3 to 9.5. Similarly the Gini coefficient drops from 0.3931 to 0.2115.

Put more formally, we find that the income-elasticity of household size is relatively high in rural Egypt. Regressing the logarithms of household size against the logarithms of income per household, using individual observations from the whole sample, we obtained the following result:

$$\log H = -1.4465 + 0.6566 \log Y$$
$$(0.0210)$$

$R^2 = 0.4312$

$n = 865$

where: H = household size

Y = total income.

This implies that household size increases very sharply with increases in household income but, none the less, since the elasticity is less than unity, the variations in household size would not generally bring about reversals in rankings of household income when these are translated into per capita terms.

An adjustment for household size was also carried out with ungrouped data. Our previous adjustment was done with grouped data, i.e. we divided the average household income of each income class by the average household size for that income group and then computed the Gini coefficient for the size-distribution of per capita income on this basis. This is a commonly used method since access to ungrouped data is not easily available for developing countries. Such a procedure, however, implicitly assumes that household size does not vary substantially *within* each income class. Where this assumption is not valid, measures of inequality based on grouped and ungrouped data can diverge significantly.

In our sample we have done the adjustment in two ways. One measure was to derive from ungrouped data the per capita income of each household, rank households by their per capita income and then compute the size-distribution of per capita income. This is equivalent to computing the distribution according to 865 income levels (i.e. the total number of households in the sample). This procedure, which we shall identify as 'ungrouped per capita income per household', yielded a value of the Gini coefficient of 0.2521, significantly higher than that obtained from using grouped data.

The alternative procedure was to obtain the per capita income for each household, to assign that income to all individuals in that household and then to rank *individuals* according to their per capita income. This procedure yielded a value of 0.3129 for the Gini coefficient, a figure substantially higher than both the previous measures.

The results of various measures of overall inequality can be summarised as follows:

	Gini coefficient
Total household income	0.3931
Total income per capita	0.2115
Ungrouped per capita income per household	0.2521
Ungrouped per capita income	0.3129

It can be seen that the standard measure of overall equality overstates the case because of variations in household size. It is also true, however, that the conventional adjustment for this phenomenon using grouped data can be strongly biased in the opposite direction and give a misleadingly low measure of overall inequality. Indeed, the 'purest' measure of per capita inequality yields a value of 0.313, which is admittedly lower than that for unadjusted total household income but not as drastically as a crude adjustment based on ungrouped data would suggest.

Inequality within Each Source of Income

The overall inequality which was discussed in the previous section could be broken down into three elements, viz. the differences in the level of earnings from each income source; the composition of total income by source of income for each household; and the degree of inequality within each source of income. We have already dealt with the first two aspects and we shall now look at the third.

Table 3.8: Distribution of 'Income Claims' by Source of Income

Source of Income	Percentage of Income Claims	Average Income per Claim (£E)	Gini Coefficient
Wages: other farms	17.9	134	0.1409
Wages: off-farm in village	9.6	188	0.2045
Wages: outside village	15.3	311	0.2167
Family farm with labour input	24.5	273	0.3295
Family farm without labour input	10.8	32	0.2316
Rent from land	3.2	84	0.1834
Rent of equipment and livestock	1.2	159	0.4555
Non-agricultural productive assets	5.7	340	0.4104
Remittances	11.8	87	0.3370

The facts are summarised in Table 3.8. It will be seen that income from labour is, predictably, the least unequally distributed. Earnings from agricultural wage-labour have a Gini coefficient of only 0.1409 while those from off-farm wage-employment (both within and outside the village) have a Gini coefficient of around 0.2. It is interesting to note that although off-farm earnings from outside the village are, on the average, substantially higher than those from wage-earnings within the village, the degree of inequality is no greater. This would suggest the existence of a 'wage-cliff' where the higher average for earnings outside the village is due to generally higher levels of wages rather than to the influence of a small number of very high earnings.

Earnings from family farm production (with labour input), the largest single source of income, are more unequally distributed. Interestingly, rent from land is fairly evenly distributed; this is in line with our earlier observation that small rental contracts predominate.

The overall degree of inequality in income distribution can be seen as the combination of two influences: the number and variety of income claims of each household, and the earnings associated with each claim. The labour supply situation of each household and the access to employment determine the number of wage earners, and access to off-farm employment outside the village is an important means to higher incomes. For most of the other sources of income, access to assets is the determining influence and income from these sources is unequally distributed, reflecting the inequality in asset distribution. We have seen the distribution of sources of income by income levels and have noted that there is a variety of income sources at even low levels of income. It was also noted, however, that incomes from land and other productive assets assumed increasing significance as we moved upwards from the poorest 30 per cent of households. It is important, therefore, to look more closely at the influence of assets in income generation and in determining overall inequality in the distribution of household incomes.

The Influence of Assets

To begin with the obvious, we note that asset ownership is strongly correlated with income and that it is very unevenly distributed, more so than income.

About 5 per cent of all households have no assets whatsoever, even given the wide definition of 'assets' that we have adopted (i.e. including the value of houses and minor livestock), and these households are concentrated in the lower income classes. Approximately 20 per cent of households in the bottom three income classes (10 per cent of all households) have no assets whatsoever, whereas the ratio falls off sharply beyond this and there are no households without assets in the top five income classes (16.3 per cent of all households).

Considering only those households which do have some assets, we find that the average value of assets owned per household rises steadily with household income, ranging from £E173 for the lowest income class to £E8,591 for the top income class. The size-distribution of total assets by household (classified according to income classes) yields a Gini coefficient of 0.723, considerably higher than that for the size-distribution of household incomes.

If we look at the matrix of asset ownership by income class (Table 3.9), several features are immediately striking. First, higher-income households have a greater diversity in their asset portfolio. Among those households which have some assets, households in the bottom three income classes have, on the average, only two types of assets while for the top income classes the corresponding figure is four. It is clear from the matrix that assets like mechanical farm equipment, transport equipment, other productive equipment, etc. are largely missing for the lowest income classes.

It is also clear that land is the dominant asset and that the incidence of its ownership increases sharply with income class. Seventy-two per cent of all households in the bottom seven income classes (bottom 50 per cent of all households) do not own any land but this percentage drops sharply to 21-25 per cent for the top three income classes (top 4.5 per cent of households). The average area and value of land owned also increases steadily with income.

It is important to note that most of the apparent relatively widespread ownership of assets among poor households is accounted for by the ownership of livestock and poultry. This conclusion emerges clearly when we take into account the fact that only about 23 per cent of households in the bottom seven income classes own land and yet land accounts for about 40 to 70 per cent of total assets owned by households in these income classes. Thus, if we leave out this minority of households which owns land in these income classes, the bulk of assets owned is accounted for by the value of 'houses'. This is true because house ownership is widespread even among the lower income classes where in each of these classes at least 70 to 80 per cent of all households own their houses. Thus the figures for the overall distribution of assets understate the degree of inequality in asset distribution to the extent that most of the apparent asset ownership among poor households is accounted for by a 'non-directly productive' asset – housing. Moreover, most of the remaining total asset ownership is accounted for by a minority of households with land and other agricultural assets within these income classes. In fact, 21 per cent had no assets other than the value of their house.

The above observations are in fact consistent with the earlier ones about the high proportion of total income that is generated by wage-employment; the large proportion of households which owns no productive assets is constrained to earn a livelihood from the sale of labour services and economic activities based on a very low level of asset ownership.

The influence of assets on income can also be seen in several other ways. The average income of those households which have no assets whatsoever is £E199, half that of households which do have assets (£E394). Similarly, among farming households which own land, an average income of £E523 is received, as compared to a corresponding figure of £E284 for those which do not own land. It is also noticeable that for households in this category, the proportion of those which do not own any land drops steadily as income increases and that the proportion is about 10 per cent or less for the top three income classes as compared to levels of 60 per cent or more in the bottom seven income classes.

A more systematic way of summarising the influence of assets on income is to regress household income against the value of assets owned by each household. The following result was obtained:

$$\log Y = -1.3923 + 0.5343 \log X$$
$$(0.0749)$$

$R^2 = 0.2854$
$n = 866$
where: Y = household income
X = value of total assets owned by the household.

The relatively low value of R^2 could be interpreted as showing that variations in total value of assets can explain 29 per cent of the total variation in incomes. This is not very surprising in view of the fact that, as we have seen, a relatively high proportion of total income comes from wages and that a significant proportion of households have few directly productive assets such as land.

It is important to note, however, that the 'elasticity coefficient' is statistically significant at the 1 per cent level of significance and its value

Table 3.9: Asset Ownership by Income Class (number of households owning each asset and average value owned per household)

Income Class (£E)	No. of House-holds	Average Size of House-hold	Land		Farm Equipment, Mechanical		Farm Equipment, Non-mechanical		Draught Animals		Other Livestock		Transport Equipment	
			No. of House-holds Owning Land	Average Value (£E)	No. of House-holds	Average Value (£E)	No. of House-holds	Average Value (£E)	No. of House-holds	Average Value (£E)	No. of House-holds	Average Value (£E)	No. of House-holds	Average Value (£E)
Less than 50.0	21	1.57	2	925	—	—	1	1	2	188	5	6	—	—
50.0-74.9	25	2.08	6	487	—	—	4	1	1	75	10	12	—	—
75.0-99.9	34	2.12	6	922	—	—	3	16	3	251	15	20	—	—
100.0-149.9	71	4.23	12	823	—	—	22	5	19	98	38	9	1	5
150.0-199.9	96	4.46	22	4 126	—	—	38	271	44	129	59	15	3	27
200.0-249.9	96	4.89	26	1 239	—	—	43	11	33	197	60	19	5	14
250.0-299.9	93	5.75	25	1 211	—	—	30	16	49	184	61	21	7	53
300.0-349.9	68	6.22	26	1 019	—	—	29	20	40	241	51	23	3	11
350.0-399.9	64	5.80	25	1 710	2	200	28	17	30	258	39	23	2	20
400.0-449.9	97	6.75	41	1 847	—	—	38	20	46	352	56	22	2	145
500.0-599.9	60	7.92	28	3 493	—	—	34	22	44	319	45	36	2	18
600.0-799.9	70	8.20	44	4 156	4	263	40	28	47	359	47	38	3	342
800.0-999.9	32	9.63	20	3 819	—	—	20	36	23	376	22	27	4	1 605
1 000.0-1 399.9	21	10.48	16	8 583	5	944	15	54	17	538	15	37	2	752
1 400.0-1 999.9	14	12.21	11	2 375	4	615	8	51	12	694	9	135	—	—
2 000 and above	4	12.50	3		1	550	2	11	2	385	2	38	—	—
Totals/averages			313	2 415	16	574	355	48	412	281	534	25	34	290

Table 3.9: Asset Ownership by Income Class (contd.)

Income Class (£E)	Productive Equipment		Sheds and Stores		Establishment		Non-agricultural Land		House		Financial Assets		Total	
	No. of Households	Average Value (£E)	No. of Households	Average Value (£E)	No. of Households	Average Value (£E)	No. of Households	Average Value (£E)	No. of Households	Average Value (£E)	No. of Households	Average Value (£E)	No. of Households	Average Value (£E)
Less than 50.0	—	—	—	—	—	—	—	—	15	49	1	−225	16	173
50.0-74.9	—	—	—	—	—	—	—	—	18	121	5	−10	22	238
75.0-99.9	2	2	1	30	1	4	3	20	25	194	10	−53	30	368
100.0-149.9	2	2	—	—	4	76	1	20	60	192	24	−27	67	347
150.0-199.9	3	22	—	—	4	46	4	35	77	231	25	−30	92	569
200.0-249.9	5	45	2	65	9	67	2	40	80	236	36	−22	94	1 432
250.0-299.9	8	64	1	100	5	233	3	40	78	363	22	−54	92	774
300.0-349.9	4	53	—	—	9	125	1	15	58	289	22	−95	67	872
350.0-399.9	—	—	1	100	10	158	1	40	59	296	22	−84	62	846
400.0-499.9	2	13	2	110	4	78	4	49	91	498	37	−10	95	1 430
500.0-599.9	6	34	1	80	6	193	1	20	54	554	15	−49	59	1 681
600.0-799.9	4	131	4	106	5	157	3	53	65	641	31	−74	70	3 111
800.0-999.9	3	61	—	—	10	1 961	—	—	31	818	15	−89	32	4 185
1 000.0-1 399.9	1	150	—	—	—	—	1	20	20	854	9	210	21	4 690
1 400.0-1 999.9	—	—	2	390	2	900	—	—	13	1 427	9	−195	14	9 076
2 000 and above	—	—	—	—	2	8 750	—	—	4	2 375	3	−391	4	8 591
Totals/average	40	14	14	133	71	522	24	36	748	409	286	−49	837	1 503

indicates that, where they do matter, assets tend to provide a powerful explanation of increases in income. A 1.00 per cent increase in the value of total assets is associated with a 0.53 per cent increase in income.

Notes

1. There are households which, according to our survey design, obtain 'farming income' from livestock and poultry but which neither own nor operate land. This source of income is relatively minor and in our subsequent discussion income from farming will refer only to income derived from the cultivation of land.

2. Rent control was introduced during the agrarian reform and still remains in force. See S. Radwan: *Agrarian reform and rural development: Egypt 1952-1975* (Geneva, ILO, 1977), Ch. 3.

3. Robert Mabro: *The Egyptian economy, 1952-1972* (Oxford, Clarendon Press, 1974), p. 207.

4. Ibid., p. 43.

5. Ibid., p. 44.

6. See D. Ghai, A. R. Khan E. Lee and S. Radwan: *Agrarian systems and rural development* (London, Macmillan, 1979), Ch. 5.

7. See D. Ghai, S. Radwan and E. Lee: 'Rural poverty in the Third World: Trends, causes and policy reorientations', Geneva, ILO, 1979, mimeographed World Employment Programme research working paper; restricted, for values of Gini coefficients for rural income distribution in other developing countries.

8. Difficulties of comparing measures of inequality based on income and consumer expenditure are well known. An attempt to reconcile the two in the case of Egypt was made in: World Bank: *Economic management in a period of transition* (Washington, DC, 1978), vol. I Annex 1.1, pp. 82-95.

4 The Structure of Asset Ownership

In the last chapter we concluded our discussion on the generation and distribution of income by looking briefly at the influence of assets on these two processes. We argued that the assets owned by households within our sample were an important but by no means complete explanation of the distribution of incomes. A central explanation for this is the nature of income generation that we analysed in the previous chapter. Since a large proportion of the income recorded in our survey comes from wages, and particularly from wages earned outside the village, it is not surprising that asset ownership did not explain more of the variation in rural incomes. Thus the inference to be drawn is not that assets are unimportant but rather that the ownership pattern of assets outside the rural economy had a significant influence on the pattern of rural incomes. Where there is a significant dependence on wage-earnings from urban employment, 'absentee' ownership of rural assets and a significant proportion of households not owning any productive assets, it is to be expected that assets owned by rural households explain only about 30 per cent of the total variation in rural incomes. Only in a closed peasant economy with no landlessness would we expect a substantially higher value for asset ownership.

It is none the less extremely important to study the structure of asset ownership in the rural economy and to link it to the pattern of income generation and distribution that we analysed in the previous chapter. The aim is to provide answers to questions such as: what are the principal forms of assets in the rural economy? Who owns what and how much? It is obvious that answers to such questions are indispensable for a complete understanding of the functioning of the rural economy and the existence of poverty.

Table 4.1 summarises the structure of assets in the rural economy. These are the aggregates of the data on the type and value of assets owned by respondent households obtained from our survey. Since it is known from independent data that apart from assets of co-operative societies and irrigation works there is virtually no corporate or communal ownership of assets in the Egyptian rural economy, we can safely assume that this aggregation of household data is an accurate reflection of the actual structure of assets.

It will be seen that assets were classified into twelve categories but that only three categories account for 93 per cent of the total value of assets. These three categories are 'land', 'house' and 'draught animals'. Land alone accounts for almost 60 per cent of the total value of assets, while draught animals account for another 9.6 per cent. Adding the other three categories of agricultural assets, we see that an over-whelming proportion of total assets, 72 per cent, is agricultural. Most of the rest of total assets is accounted for by the value of houses owned, constituting 24 per cent of total assets.

The remaining five categories of assets – transport equipment, other productive assets, sheds and stores, business establishments and non-agricultural land – accounted for only 4 per cent of the total value of assets.

Thus the structure of assets, unlike the pattern of income generation, is heavily concentrated in the form of assets related to agricultural production. Excluding the value of housing, 95 per cent of productive assets are agricultural.

Table 4.1:   The Structure of Assets

	Total Value (£E)	% of Total Non-Financial	No. of House-holders Owning	Average Value
Land	753 751	59.30	313	2 406
Farm equipment mechanical	9 180	0.72	16	574
Farm equipment non-mechanical	17 079	1.34	355	48
Draught animals	122 048	9.59	415	294
Other livestock	13 284	1.04	534	25
Transport equipment	10 636	0.84	45	236
Other productive equipment	577	0.05	40	14
Sheds and stores	1 862	0.15	14	133
Establishment	37 060	2.91	71	522
Non-agricultural land	870	0.07	24	36
House	305 431	24.03	749	408
Financial assets	−14 267	—	288	50
Total	1 257 511	—	838	
Total non-financial	1 271 778	100.00	834	1 525

This structure of assets can also be analysed in terms of the number of households in our sample which own each type of asset and the average value of ownership per household of each asset. The average value of total assets among the 834 households that do own some asset is

£E1,523. There is, however, much variation in terms of the spread and average value of ownership of each asset. Only 313 households (36 per cent of the total) own land, but the average value of land owned is very high, £E2,406. In sharp contrast, only very small proportions of all households own the five items of non-agricultural assets other than a house. No more than 8 per cent of the total number of households own any of these items and the average value owned is, moreover, extremely low, ranging from £E14 in the case of 'other productive equipment' to £E522 in the case of 'establishment'. Most of the remaining categories of assets are, however, characterised by a relatively wide dispersion of ownership and a low average value of ownership. For example, 534 households (62 per cent) own 'other livestock', but the average value of ownership is only £E25 per household and 749 households own a house of an average value of £E408.

To complete this summary picture of ownership of assets it is necessary to note the degree of inequality in the ownership of the main assets (Table 4.2). The Gini coefficient for the size-distribution of total

Table 4.2:   The Size-distribution of Assets

	Gini Coefficient
Total assets	0.7254
Total assets, excluding financial	0.7205
Agricultural assets, excluding land	0.5413
Land – value	0.5792
Land – area	0.5558
Non-agricultural assets	0.5160

assets (excluding financial assets) is 0.721. The top 5.6 per cent of households own 47 per cent of the total value of assets. The coefficient for the main categories of assets taken separately, is, however, lower: the Gini coefficient for land is 0.579, that for agricultural assets other than land is 0.541 and that for all remaining assets is 0.516. This implies that differential access to assets of greatly differing values is a more important cause of the overall inequality in asset distribution than the inequality in the distribution of each asset *per se*. To see the pattern of differential access to assets and the relationship of asset 'portfolios' to the total value of assets owned, we show in Table 4.3 the structure of asset ownership classified by classes of the total value of assets owned.

The pattern revealed in this table is essentially the same as that of the matrix of asset ownership by income groups discussed in the previous

Table 4.3:   The Structure of Assets by Asset Class (totals)

Asset Class (£E)	Land		Farm Machinery, Mechanical		Farm Machinery, Non-mechanical		Draught Animals		Other Livestock		Transport Equipment		Other Productive Equipment	
	No. of Households	Value (£E)	No. of Households	Value (£E)	No. of Households	Value (£E)	No. of Households	Value (£E)	No. of Households	Value (£E)	No. of Households	Value (£E)	No. of Households	Value (£E)
0	2	365	—	—	5	6	3	275	9	199	—	—	1	20
1.0-49.9	—	—	—	—	11	18	6	455	40	389	3	75	2	24
50.0-99.9	—	—	—	—	15	38	12	640	22	137	5	170	2	41
100.0-149.9	1	80	—	—	17	61	14	1 140	41	521	2	45	6	49
150.0-199.9	1	200	1	200	15	43	13	1 000	30	409	1	80	—	—
200.0-299.9	4	835	—	—	30	179	31	3 623	51	1 149	5	243	3	24
300.0-399.9	10	2 705	—	—	15	128	26	3 614	38	1 034	3	160	4	13
400.0-599.9	22	7 000	—	—	29	272	46	9 605	48	938	1	15	1	1
600.0-799.9	20	8 370	1	200	23	257	27	5 663	33	623	1	3	—	—
800.0-999.9	18	8 440	—	—	16	216	21	4 787	25	1 010	5	1 090	4	55
1 000.0-1 499.9	37	27 880	—	—	28	707	39	9 869	43	949	2	75	4	44
1 500.0-1 999.9	42	49 811	—	—	30	536	37	9 704	31	682	8	1 795	4	38
2 000.0-2 999.9	63	101 792	3	1 120	46	1 174	55	20 857	49	1 501	3	185	4	98
3 000.0-4 999.9	44	109 218	2	500	36	1 198	42	21 475	39	1 430	4	3 600	4	167
5 000.0 and above	49	437 055	9	7 160	39	12 246	43	29 341	35	2 313	2	3 100	1	3
Total	313	753 751	16	9 180	355	17 079	415	122 048	534	13 284	45	10 636	40	577
Percentage of total assets		59.91		0.73		1.35		9.70		1.05		0.85		0.05

Table 4.3: The Structure of Assets by Asset Class (totals) (contd.)

Asset Class (£E)	Sheds and Stores		Establishment		Non-agricultural		House		Financial		Total	
	No. of Households	Value (£E)	No. of Households	Value (£E)	No. of Households	Value (£E)	No. of Households	Value (£E)	No. of Households	Value (£E)	No. of Households	Value (£E)
0	—	—	—	—	—	—	7	505	17	-2 183	16	813[a]
1.0-49.9	—	—	5	74	—	—	43	1 897	16	-1 144	70	1 788
50.0-99.9	—	—	6	174	2	40	46	3 265	11	-29	56	4 476
100.0-149.9	—	—	5	340	5	120	74	8 513	22	-527	81	10 342
150.0-199.9	—	—	5	345	—	—	44	6 795	11	-428	48	8 444
200.0-299.9	—	—	7	336	3	100	66	12 120	29	-914	75	17 895
300.0-399.9	1	20	5	282	4	180	57	13 205	14	-625	59	20 696
400.0-599.9	1	30	11	1 622	1	80	69	18 480	25	-1 090	75	36 983
600.0-799.9	—	—	3	251	1	60	41	16 316	17	-830	44	30 743
800.0-999.9	1	30	6	1 370	2	40	41	20 820	19	-262	42	37 776
1 000.0-1 499.9	1	100	3	801	1	40	55	30 280	13	-449	57	69 126
1 500.0-1 999.9	4	222	1	900	2	30	47	20 915	22	-1 070	48	83 441
2 000.0-2 999.9	2	280	5	3 020	2	100	66	43 320	27	-436	76	172 953
3 000.0-4 999.9	4	1 180	3	3 000	—	—	46	38 350	17	-2 926	47	176 292
5 000.0 and above			6	24 505	1	80	47	70 950	28	-1 050	50	586 879
Total	14	1 862	71	37 060	24	870	749	305 731	288	-14 267	844	1 257 811
Percentage of total assets		0.15		2.94		0.07		24.30		-1.10		

Notes: a. Negative asset position.
b. Negative percentage.

chapter. There are three features of interest to note. First, households with a low level of total assets (less than £E200), comprising 27 per cent of all households with assets, have the value of the house as the overwhelming part of their total assets. Moreover, they own virtually no land and have a very limited diversity in their asset holdings. Secondly, land assumes increasing importance as a proportion of total assets as we move up the asset classes. For those with assets of between £E200 and £E1,500, land accounts for at least one-third of the total value of assets and this increases to over 50 per cent for households with more than £E1,500 worth of assets. Thirdly, there is a greater diversity in asset holdings as we move up the asset value classes.

Table 4.4: The Structure of Assets for Households with Land Ownership and Those without

	Households with Land Ownership			Households without Land Ownership		
	No.	Value (£E)	Average Value (£E)	No.	Value (£E)	Average Value (£E)
Land	313	753 751	2 403	—	—	—
Farm equipment, mechanical	15	8 980	599	—	—	—
Farm equipment, non-mechanical	221	16 120	73	134	959	7
Draught animals	249	91 343	367	166	30 705	185
Other livestock	224	7 090	32	310	6 194	20
Transport equipment	17	4 285	252	28	6 351	227
Other productive equipment	13	332	26	27	245	9
Sheds and stores	13	1 842	142	1	20	20
Establishment	15	15 695	1 046	56	21 365	382
Non-agricultural land	5	210	42	19	660	35
House	295	171 290	581	454	134 441	296
Financial assets	137	−11 398	−83	151	−2 869	−19
Total assets	313	1 059 540	3 385	525	198 271	378
Total farming assets excluding land	288	123 533	428	377	33 058	101
Total non-agricultural assets	306	182 256	596	495	160 213	324
Total non-financial assets	313	1 070 938	3 422	521	201 140	386

Note: 'Establishment' refers to any premises, other than the house, which are used by the household for any industrial, commercial or service activity.

Table 4.5: Sources of Income for Households with Landholdings and Those without

Source of Income	With Landholdings			Without Landholdings		
	No. of Income Claims	Total Value (£E)	Average Value (£E)	No. of Income Claims	Total Value (£E)	Average Value (£E)
Wages: other farms	156	18 903	121	149	21 942	147
Wages: off-farm in village	56	10 400	186	108	20 482	190
Wages: off-farm out of village	109	35 946	329	152	45 398	298
Earnings from family farm	426	115 171	270	218	3 888[b]	18
Rent of land	24	1 385	58	30	3 150	105
Rent of equipment	21	3 334	159	—	—	—
Earnings from non-agricultural assets	19	8 520	449	79	24 785	314
Rental of house	2	324	162	—	—	—
Remittances	62	5 905	95	139	11 497	83

Notes: [a] There were 427 households with landholdings and 440 households without landholdings. The average household income for these two groups was £E471 and £E310 respectively.
b. Livestock and poultry.

Characteristics of Various Categories of Asset-owning Households

We have seen that land is by far the dominant part of total assets in rural Egypt and in this section we shall therefore examine the differences between households which own land and those which do not. This would take us further in establishing the type and magnitude of the influence that the ownership of assets has on the distribution of income.

Tables 4.4 and 4.5 set out the differences in terms of asset ownership and sources of income between households which own land and those which do not. Average income at £E471 is substantially higher for the group of landowning households and, whilst they constitute only one-third of all households, they own 84 per cent of the total value of assets. The average value of total assets of landowning households of £E3,422 is almost nine times higher than that of households which do not own land. There are also striking variations in the composition of assets of each group. Eighty per cent of the total assets of landed families are agricultural assets while another 16 per cent are accounted for by the value of housing. Thus all other assets make up only 4 per cent of the total, an indication of the very limited diversity in the asset structure of most landed households. This can also be seen in the fact that not more than 5 per cent of these households have any non-agricultural assets other than a house. It is also of interest to note that only 5 per cent of all landed households have any item of mechanised farm equipment.

For households not owning land, we find that two-thirds of the total value of assets are accounted for by the value of housing. The remaining assets are accounted for by non-agricultural productive assets, 17.3 per cent of the total, and agricultural assets (mainly draught animals and livestock) which accounted for 19 per cent of total assets. it is noteworthy that other than for 'house' and 'other livestock', the spread of ownership of other assets is very restricted, especially for non-agricultural productive assets. Only for 'establishment', which is owned by 10.7 per cent of households in this category, does the spread of ownership exceed 6 per cent of all households. Thus, only a small minority of 'landless' households have any meaningful alternative asset. Moreover, the average values of these non-agricultural productive assets are very low, not exceeding £E400. They are also lower than the values of the corresponding assets that are owned by landed families. Particularly striking is the difference in the case of the category 'establishment'; the average value in the case of landed families is £E1,046, while for non-landed families it is only £E382.

It is clear, therefore, that the ownership of land constitutes a fissure in the asset structure which separates the asset-rich from the asset-poor. It is also clear that the ownership of non-agricultural productive assets does not provide as sharp a dividing line in the distribution of assets.

Table 4.6: Sources of Income of Households Owning 'Establishment', 'Transport Equipment' and 'Other Productive Equipment'

Source of Income	No. of Households	Total Income	Average Income per Income Claim
		(£E)	(£E)
Wages: other farms	36	4 567	127
Wages: off-farm in village	30	5 987	200
Wages: outside village	47	12 549	265
Family farm	105	9 550	91
Rent from land	12	651	54
Rent : equipment and livestock	2	105	52
Non-agricultural productive assets	87	30 451	350
Rental of house	1	300	300
Remittances	19	1 660	87
Totals/average	339	65 930	464

Note: There were 142 households which owned one or more of these categories of assets (i.e. 'establishment', 'transport equipment' and 'other productive equipment'). The total value of assets owned by these households was £E196,512 and the total income was £E65,930. The mean income of these households was £E464 and the mean value of assets was £E1,384.

This can be seen in Table 4.6, which separates all these households which own 'establishment', 'transport equipment' and 'other productive equipment'. There are only 142 households (16 per cent of all households) which fall into this category and the average value of assets of this group is less than half of that of the landowning group (it should be noted that the former group itself includes some households which own land). The pattern of income sources also points to the relative unimportance of income from non-agricultural assets even among this group. Only 46 per cent of total income comes from 'earnings from non-agricultural assets', whereas 34 per cent comes from wages. Although the average household income of £E464 for this group is higher than that for the whole sample, we know that income from non-agricultural productive assets is very unequally distributed; 70 per cent of earnings from this source are less than £E300 per earner. There is thus only a very small minority of households deriving high incomes from such assets and the rest belong to the petty-producing rural sector.

Land and Income

Land is the primary asset but, as we have seen in the earlier chapter, income derived directly from the operation of land accounts for only 36 per cent of total income generated in the rural economy, with wages from agricultural labour accounting for another 12 per cent. The next logical step in the analysis would thus be to look more closely at the distribution of land ownership and the incidence of landlessness among rural households.

We know that only 36 per cent of households in our sample own any land and that only 49.3 per cent have a landholding. We could thus say, at one level, that just over half of rural households do not have access to land and equate the 'landless' in this sense with the rural poor. This is not, however, a very meaningful classification.

Table 4.7:   Distribution of Land Ownership

Size of Land Ownership (kirats)	No. of Households	Average Area (kirats)	Total Area (kirats)
Less than 24.0	174	12.9	2 253
24.0-47.9	60	41.1	2 467
48.0-71.9	33	63.8	2 106
72.0-95.9	21	88.3	1 854
96.0-119.9	7	113.4	794
120.0-143.9	7	139.6	977
144.0-167.9	2	158.0	316
168.0-191.9	1	173.0	173
192.0-239.9	1	231.0	231
240.0-359.9	4	337.5	1 350
360.0-479.9	2	398.0	796
More than 480.0	1	600.0	600
Totals/average	313	44.5	13 917

If we look at the size-distribution of land ownership in Table 4.7 we find that there is an overwhelming preponderance of very small ownerships: 21.7 per cent of all landownerships are less than half a feddan in size, while 39 per cent are under 1 feddan in size. From the data on farm production in Table 4.8 we know that the income derived

Table 4.8: Value of Farm Production by Size of Landholding

Size of Landholding (kirats)	(1) No. of Households	(2) Average Holding Size (kirats)	(3) Average Cropping Area (kirats)	(4) Average Household Size	(5) Average Value of Net Farm Output (£E)	(6) Average Total Household Income (£E)	(7) = (5)÷(6) (%)
Less than 3.0	5	2.8	5.6	6.0	32	399	8.0
3.0-5.9	34	5.3	10.3	5.5	68	339	20.2
6.0-11.9	56	10.1	19.4	6.1	99	336	29.6
12.0-17.9	26	16.1	30.2	5.5	147	362	40.6
18.0-23.9	47	22.7	38.6	6.8	156	340	45.8
24.0-29.9	28	28.4	50.9	6.7	265	442	60.1
30.0-35.9	41	34.8	63.2	6.3	241	412	58.5
36.0-41.9	15	40.4	68.5	7.6	310	453	68.5
42.0-47.9	43	47.6	78.0	6.6	288	426	67.7
48.0-59.9	30	56.9	88.5	6.8	327	419	78.1
60.0-71.9	40	69.9	112.9	8.2	314	542	58.0
72.0-95.9	29	88.2	128.6	8.4	523	643	81.3
96.0-119.9	10	111.3	167.9	9.9	696	1 047	66.5
120.0-191.9	12	154.3	195.6	10.6	594	950	62.5
192.0-480.0	11	340.4	500.2	13.2	902	1 314	68.6
Total/average	427	48.9					

Note: Average value of net farm output is defined as (value of sales + imputed value of non-consumption) − (total production costs, including value of non-produced inputs but excluding imputed value of family labour).

from farming *per se* is low in relation to either average household income or the poverty-line income.

For farms of less than 1 feddan in size, the net value of farm output is very low, ranging from an average £E32 for the less than 3 kirat farms to £E155 for the 18-24 kirat group. The range in the net value of farm output is enormous, 28 times. Moreover, only households with landholdings of more than 3 feddans (or 72 kirats) have a level of income from farming alone (i.e. net value of farm output) which exceeds either average household income for our sample as a whole or the poverty line income. Such households constitute only 14.5 per cent of all households with landholdings and only 7.2 per cent of all households in our sample. Strikingly, however, the variation in total household income within this group of households (when classified according to the size of the landholding) is very much smaller. The range is only 3.3, total income is not a monotonic function of holding size and for no group is the total household income less than £E335 (the mean household income for all families with landholdings is £E471). This much greater equality in the distribution of income arises from the much higher proportion of total income derived from off-farm income sources for households with very small landholdings. For households in the less than 1 feddan category, the proportion of net value of farm output to total household income ranges from 8 per cent to 46 per cent. This proportion is much higher in the higher landholding classes, but for the entire group of households with landholdings, the net farming income is only 57 per cent of total income. These results point to the fact that it would be wrong to take the distribution of landholding size as a proxy for the distribution of income, since non-farm sources of income have a very strong equalising effect.

Since we cannot assume that a small size of landholding is necessarily associated with poverty, the presumption thus shifts back to the fact that the poor are concentrated in the 'landless' category. It is true that the average income of this group is less than two-thirds that of households with landholdings, but this is a heterogeneous group in terms of occupational structure. In the first place, we cannot define the 'landless' simply by reference to the occupation of the household head. As shown in Table 4.9, there is a significant number of households with landholdings whose heads are in non-agricultural occupations. Of the 427 households listed as having landholdings, only 318 have the occupation of the household head listed as 'farmer'. The rest have their landholdings run either as the secondary occupation of the household head or by other members of the household.

Table 4.9:   Incidence of Poverty by Type of Household

A Incidence of Poverty among Agricultural and Non-agricultural Households

	Mean Income (£E)	% Households below £E300
1. Households with landholdings (427 households)	472.2	36.3
2. Households without landholdings (439 households)	299.6	64.0
3. Non-agricultural households (all households where the main occupation of the head is neither 'farmer' nor 'farm labourer') (436 households)	366.0	51.6
3(a). Households in 3 with landholdings (100)	519.0	29.0
3(b). Households in 3 without landholdings (336)	320.0	58.3

B. Characteristics of Part-time Farmers (main occupation of household head not 'farmer' but the household is operating a farm)

Occupation of Household Head	No. of Households	Average Income (£E)	Average Income Total Sample (£E)
Housewife	26	415	(269)
Agricultural labourer	11	353	(239)
Craftsman or industrial worker	11	694	(396)
Construction	1	494	(370)
Service	6	696	(413)
Government employee	34	519	(446)
Others	3	507	(343)
Disabled	16	508	(266)
Regular army	1	823	(579)
National service	1	443	(405)
Student	1	342	
Total/average	111	503	

Various categories thus need to be identified to get a full interpretation of 'landless':

(i)   Families with 'farming' as the main occupation of the household head: this group covers 36.7 per cent of the total sample and 80 per cent of all those in these households who are in the labour force work on the family farm. Another 4 per cent work as labourers on other farms while the remaining 15 per cent work in non-agricultural occupations.

(ii)   Households headed by landless agricultural labourers: this is the true landless population and it comprises 13 per cent of all households and 26 per cent of agricultural households (households where the occupation of the head is 'farmer' or 'farm labourer'). For these households 82 per cent of all individuals in the labour force are farm labourers.

(iii)   Households headed by persons with a non-agricultural occupation: 50 per cent of all households fall into this category, but the important feature to note is that 24 per cent of these households operate a farm. Indeed, almost a quarter of all landholdings are operated by household heads whose main occupation is not in agricultural employment and 21 per cent of all individual in the labour force within this group of households have agricultural occupations.

Table 4.10:   Incidence of Poverty by Occupation of Household Head

Occupation	No.	Average Income (£E)	% below £E300
Housewife	74	269	71.6
Farmer	318	460	37.4
Agricultural labourer	112	239	82.1
Craftsman	60	396	41.6
Construction worker	19	370	26.2
Service	61	413	44.2
Government employee	105	446	42.9
Others	48	343	58.3
Disabled	55	266	69.0
Regular army	3	579	—
National service	8	405	—

The characteristics of the above three groups show that there is considerable overlap in terms of economic activity and that 'landlessness' needs to be carefully defined. We can say unambiguously that households in group (ii) are landless since they conform to one standard definition of landlessness ('that part of the agricultural population without access to land') and it is also the group with the lowest average income (cf. Table 4.10). Group (iii), however, is problematic. It includes: (a) those households which have some land but where the family farm is only a minor part of total household activity; (b) those households where earnings from the family farm constitute a major part of total income notwithstanding the fact that the main occupation of the household head is non-agricultural (we know from qualitative data gained during the enumeration that this includes cases such as a govenment employee supervising a fairly large family farm as his secondary occupation); and (c) households which are totally non-agricultural. Ideally, we would define as 'landless' only those in group (c) who are marginalised erstwhile peasants or have been frustrated in their attempt to gain access to land. For such households which, to coin a term, we could call the 'disguised landless', their present economic activity would be the result of 'push' factors emanating from the agrarian system and we would expect them to be among the rural poor. The rest, however, can be considered neither landless nor necessarily poor.

Unfortunately, we have no information to identify the landless according to such criteria. We can, however, analyse the distribution of income and the incidence of poverty to establish the extent of the congruence between poverty and 'landlessness' in the broad sense of 'not-operating a farm'.

There are important differences in income and the incidence of poverty when households are classified according to main occupation (Table 4.10). For households with 'farming' as the main occupation of the household head, the mean income is £E460 and the incidence of poverty is relatively low, 37.4 per cent. In contrast, households headed by landless labourers have a much lower mean income (£E239) and a substantially higher incidence of poverty (82.1 per cent). For the remainig households, i.e. those whose heads have non-agricultural main occupations, the mean income and incidence of poverty were £E366 and 51.6 per cent respectively. There are, however, significant differences within this latter group. Households headed by housewives and disabled persons, which comprise 15 per cent of all households, have mean incomes and an incidence of poverty which are only slightly better than those for households headed by agricultural labourers. For other households, which are headed by persons in wage- or self-employment, the incidence of poverty is in the region of 40 per cent.

An alternative split of these non-agricultural households yields interesting results. As we noted earlier, 24 per cent of households headed by a person in a non-agricultural occupation do in fact operate a farm. The mean income of such households is substantially higher than for the other non-agricultural households (£E519 compared to £E320) and the incidence of poverty is much lower (29 per cent instead of 58 per cent). Thus, access to land is associated with higher incomes even for households in the 'non-agricultural' category.

A closer look at the category of households operating a farm but which are headed by a person with a non-agricultural main occupation reveals some interesting features (Table 4.9B). A breakdown of such households by main occupation of the head shows that 31 per cent of them are headed by 'government employees' and another 23 per cent are headed by 'housewives'. The relative incidence of farm operation among these two categories of households is in fact substantially higher than for households headed by persons in other occupations. It is also interesting to note that, in all occupational categories, the average income of households that have a landholding is significantly higher than the average for each occupational category as a whole.

The case of households headed by 'housewives' operating a farm can probably be accounted for by the sociology of household structure. The head in these households is probably a matriach who is not economically active and the operation of farms could thus be in the hands of other members of the household. The case of households headed by 'government employees' is, however, more intriguing. Almost one-third of all such households operate a farm and this phenomenon could be indicative either of the fact that government salaries provide the means of gaining access to land or that it is the children of landed families who have had a higher probability of gaining access to government employment. Unfortunately, our survey results do not enable us to pursue this line of inquiry.

Tenancy

We have so far discussed the distribution of land ownership and the distribution of landholdings without attempting to link the two distributions in any way. In order to do this it will be necessary to examine the rental market in land and the various types of tenancy.

It will be recalled that in the previous chapter we had remarked on the very small proportion of total income that came from rent and we had hypothesised that this was due both to the limited extent of the rental market in land and the low rental values. We shall therefore first proceed to check on the validity of this hypothesis by looking at what is revealed on tenancy relationships from the data gathered on farming operations.

The first thing to note is that the rental market is far more significant than what was originally suggested by the examination of sources of

Table 4.11: Land Tenancy

Size of Landholding (kirats)	Area Owned			Area Rented in[a]			Area Rent out[b]			Net Holding			% of Net Holding Rented in	% of Net Holding Rented out
	Households	Average Area	Total Area	Households	Average Area	Total Area	Households	Average Area	Total Area	Households	Average Area	Total Area		
0[c]	33	51.6	1 704	2	22.5	45	35	50.0	1 749	—	—	—	—	100.0
Less than 24.0	86	13.4	1 151	113	12.7	1 435	8	34.8	278	168	13.4	2 255	63.6	24.2
24.0–47.9	83	27.6	2 288	103	27.9	2 875	6	47.7	286	127	38.4	4 877	58.6	12.5
48.0–71.9	53	47.9	2 542	46	44.7	2 055	5	18.2	91	70	64.4	4 506	45.6	3.6
72.0–95.9	27	58.0	1 567	19	52.2	991	—	—	—	29	88.2	2 558	38.7	—
96.0–119.9	10	91.0	910	8	49.9	399	3	65.3	196	10	111.3	1 113	35.9	21.5
120.0–143.9	5	113.8	569	3	96.0	288	—	—	—	6	142.8	857	33.6	—
144.0–167.9	4	107.0	428	4	99.0	396	—	—	—	5	164.8	824	48.1	—
168.0–191.9	1	34.0	34	1	136.0	136	—	—	—	1	170.0	170	80.0	—
192.0–239.9	2	220.5	441	1	120.0	120	1	120.0	120	2	220.5	441	27.2	27.2
240.0–359.9	3	270.0	810	1	168.0	168	—	—	—	3	326.0	978	17.2	—
360.0–480.0	6	245.5	1 473	5	180.0	900	1	48.0	48	6	387.5	2 325	38.7	3.3
Total/average	313	44.5	13 917	306	32.1	9 808	59	—	2 768	427	—	20 904	46.9	13.2

Notes: a. 'Rented in' = land hired by the household.
b. 'Rented out' = land hired by the household to others.
c. Two households rented in lands which were then rented out again.

income (Table 4.11). Forty-seven per cent of the total land area operated within our sample was rented and almost 20 per cent of the total land owned in our sample was let.

In speaking of aggregates derived from the data in our sample, it is important to bear in mind that for many economic relationships we are not referring to a closed system. Thus, in analysing the rental market, it is clear that the 'origins' and 'destinations' of a rental arrangement can be fairly complicated. There are three basic types of relationships relating to the renting that can be identified:

(i)   a tenant renting from another household in our sample;
(ii) a tenant renting from a landlord outside the sample but who resides in the villages covered by the survey; and
(iii) a tenant renting from an absentee landlord who resides outside the village and is thus otuside our sample.

Furthermore, combinations of these relationships are possible, e.g. a household renting some land from another household in the sample and some land from an absentee landlord. It should also be clear that analogous relationships exist in the case of the letting of land.

With these clarificiations in mind, we can proceed to analyse some characteristics of tenancy relationships. In our sample, there were 306 households which rented some land. As should be clear from our discussion in the previous section, not all of these households had farming as either the main occupation of the hosuehold head or for whom agriculture was the main economic activity. Thus, although we could say that 72 per cent of all households with a landholding rented some land, it is also true that only 57 per cent of all households whose head was 'running a family farm' as the main occupation rented land. This suggests that the incidence of renting is much higher among households where farming is not the primary economic activity.

The most striking fact about the tenancy relationships is that almost half of all tenancies are from absentee landlords who reside outside the village, and that 57 per cent of the total area rented comes from this source. The average area rented from absentee landlords of 35.9 kirats is also higher than the average of 27.2 kirats for land rented from landlords within the village. This pattern of rentals explains away some of the discrepancy between the low proportion of rent in total income (observed earlier) and the fact that almost half of the total operated area was rented in.

The size-distribution of rentals by the area involved also varies between the two sources: 45 per cent of all tenancies from landlords resident in the village are of under half a feddan in size while the corresponding figure from absentee landlords is 24 per cent. There is also a much higher incidence of large tenancies of over 10 feddans from absentee landlords (3.3 per cent of all such tenancies) than from landlords in the village (1.3 per cent of all such tenancies).

The various types of tenancy relationships and levels of rent can be seen in Table 4.12. The overwhelmingly dominant type of tenancy is cash rental; 92 per cent of all tenancies (89 per cent of the total area rented) were under this arrangement. Share-cropping on the half-share basis accounted for another 7 per cent of tenancies and 6.7 per cent of the total area rented, while 'other share-cropping' accounted for the rest. The average area rented did not vary significantly between cash rental and share-cropping on the half-share basis. The average level of rent paid did vary substantially: £E42.30 in the case of cash rental and £E77.70 in the case of share-cropping. Expressed in terms of rent paid per kirat of land rented, the figures became £E1.39 and £E2.50 respectively. The cost of renting under a share-cropping arrangement is thus on average 80 per cent higher than renting for cash.

· The level of rents is, however, very low in relation to the average value of land obtained from the survey; the average value cash rent per kirat was only 2.4 per cent of the average value of land per kirat and the corresponding figure for share-cropping rents was 4.25 per cent.

Land Movements

A central issue in an agrarian society characterised by the private ownership of land is the process of change in the pattern of land ownership. Ownership is transferred in two basic ways: an intra-family transfer through inheritance or by the process of accumulation and decumulation brought about by market forces. Both these ways of transferring ownership can be expected to lead to growing concentration in land ownership. Inheritance contributes to the impoverishment of the peasantry through the extreme fragmentation of land it brings about under conditions of population pressure while a highly unequal initial distribution of land generates further disequalising forces through the process of asset loss by the poor and asset acquisition by the rich.

Our survey, therefore, included a section designed to capture these relationships. Respondents were asked questions about their personal history of land ownership: whether they ever owned land, how much,

Table 4.12: Tenancy Arrangements

Households Renting out Land	Cash Rent	Share-cropping (half)	Mortgage	Total
No. of households	46	10	3	
Area rented out (kirats)	2 227	515	26	
Total value of rent received (£E)	13 250	1 431	15	
	No. of Households Renting out for Cash	No. of Households Renting out under Share-cropping	No. of Households Renting out under Mortgage	Total
Size-distribution of area rented out under each arrangement (kirats)				
Less than 6.0	8	1	2	11
6.0-11.9	13	1	1	15
12.0-23.9	6	—	—	6
24.0-47.9	8	5	—	13
48.0-96.0	5	1	—	6
120.0	4	2	—	6
132.0	1	—	—	1
600.0	1	—	—	1
Size-distribution of value of rent received (£E)				
Less than 10.0	10	—	3	13
10.0-19.9	12	—	—	12
20.0-59.9	9	2	—	11
60.0-99.9	7	2	—	9
100.0-149.9	3	2	—	5
150.0-199.9	2	3	—	5
200.0-400.0	1	1	—	2
800.0	1	—	—	1
10 150.0	1	—	—	1

Table 4.12: Tenancy Arrangements (contd)

Households Renting in Land	Cash Rent	Share-cropping (half)	Share-cropping (other)	Total
No. of households	276	21	2	299
Total area rented in (kirats)	8 638	654	432	9 724
Total rent paid (£E)	12 364	1 322	1 652	15 338
Size-distribution of value of rent paid (£E)				
Less than 10	27	2	—	
11-20	64	2	—	
21-30	56	3	—	
31-50	49	4	—	
51-80	47	5	—	
81-100	17	—	—	
101-150	9	1	—	
151-200	4	4	—	
201-290	3	—	—	
600	—	—	1	
1 002	—	—	1	

Size-distribution of rentals from resident and absentee landlords (kirats)	Landlord Resident in Village	Absentee Landlord
Less than 24.0	84	80
24.0-47.9	38	42
48.0-71.9	11	20
72.0-95.9	4	3
96.0-167.9	1	4
168.0	1	2
Total	139	151

how the land was obtained, and details of any land lost. The reference periods were the lifetime of the resopndent, the last five years preceding enumeration and the last year preceding enumeration. The results of this section of the survey generally confirm the expectation that land transfers have had a net disequalising effect. The data enable us to establish the relative influence of inheritance and other factors in determining the current land ownership position. Fitting a simple linear equation to measure the correlation between current land ownership and the amount of land acquired through inheritance yields the following results:

$$Y = 1.087 + 0.7952X$$
$$\quad\;\; (5.362)\;(0.0282)$$
$$R^2 = 0.6324$$
$$n = 313$$

where: Y = current land ownership in kirats of the ith household
   X = amount of land in kirats inherited by the ith household.

As expected, inheritance is the major determinant of current land ownership but what is particularly interesting is that about one-third of the variation in current ownership remains unexplained and can be attributed to other mechanisms of land transfer.

A total of 323 households (37.3 per cent of all households) responded 'yes' to the question of whether or not they had ever owned land during the lifetime of the household head. Of these households, 14.6 per cent reported that they had acquired some land through purchase while 12.1 per cent reported that they had received some land through the provisions of the agrarian reform laws. On the other side of the ledger, 3.4 per cent of households which had ever owned land reported that they had lost some land through forfeiture while another 7.4 per cent reported some loss of land through sales. Although it should be noted that these categories of land transfer are not mutually exclusive (i.e. the households which lost land through 'forfeiture' could also be the same households which sold land, etc), these figures do indicate that the incidence of land transfers other than through inheritance is fairly significant. We could say categorically that at least 14.6 per cent of all households which ever owned land reported land purchase, while 7.4 per cent reported sales. The amount of land involved in these transactions was also relatively high; 19.3 per cent of total area currently owned had been obtained through purchase.

To gauge the impact of these land transactions on inequality in land

Table 4.13: Land Lost: by Size of Land Ownership

Land Owned (kirats)	Sale			Forfeiture			Others		Total		
	No.	Area	Average	No.	Area	Average	No.	Area	No.	Area	Average
0	16	256	16.0	—	—	—	—	—	16	256	16.0
0.1-23.9	5	31	6.2	4	31	7.8	1	24	10	86	8.6
24.0-47.9	1	12	12.0	2	18	9.0	—	—	3	30	10.0
48.0-71.9	2	12	6.0	2	17	8.5	1	9	5	38	7.6
72.0-95.9	—	—	—	1	14	14.0	—	—	1	14	14.0
96.0-119.9	—	—	—	1	2	2.0	—	—	1	2	2.0
120.0-167.9	—	—	—	—	—	—	—	—	—	—	—
168.0-192.0	—	—	—	1	24	24.0	—	—	1	24	24.0
Total/average	24	311	12.96	11	106	9.64	2	33	37	450	12.16

ownership, it will be necessary to examine their distribution by land ownership and income classes. As shown in Tables 4.13 and 4.14, when classified by the current land ownership of those households involved, these transactions have been highly disequalising. In the case of the loss of land through sales and forfeiture we find that the incidence of loss has been overwhelmingly concentrated on the small landowners. Of all households which reported some loss of land 43 per cent are now completely landless and, since the average amount of land lost was small (only 16 kirats), it is safe to conclude that most of these households had previously belonged to the 'less than 24 kirat' category. Another 27 per cent of households which lost land now own less than 24 kirats. By contrast, there was only one case of land loss coming from the 'more than 120 kirat' (i.e. 5 feddan) category. In terms of the total amount of land lost, we find that 76 per cent of the total area lost came from households in the 'less than 24 kirat category' (including those which are now landless), whereas only 17.3 per cent of total current land ownership falls within this ownership category. Thus we see that land loss has been overwhelmingly concentrated on very small farmers and has therefore contributed to a worsening of the distribution of land ownership.

Table 4.14:   Land Purchased by Size of Land Ownership

Land Ownership (kirats)	No. of Owners	No. Who Purchased Land	Area Purchased (kirats)	Present Total Ownership (kirats)
Less than 24.0	174	12	120	2 253
24.0-47.9	60	11	354	2 467
48.0-71.9	33	8	284	2 106
72.0-95.9	21	6	293	1 854
96.0-119.9	7	1	60	794
120.0-143.9	7	2	120	977
144.0-167.9	2	0	—	—
168.0-191.9	1	1	130	173
192.0-239.9	1	1	111	231
240.0-359.9	4	3	636	1 350
360.0-479.9	2	2	576	796
480.0 and above	1	0	—	—
Total	313	47	2 684	13 001

In principle, of course, land lost has to be balanced against land gained and it is only after we have determined the net change that we can judge the overall impact on land distribution. The data on land purchases, however, sweep away this doubt; they show the inverse relationship to that for land loss. In Table 4.14, we can see the relative incidence of land purchases of each land ownership class (i.e. the number of households reporting a purchase divided by the number of households in that land ownership class). It is clear that the incidence rises sharply with the size of land ownership. Only 7 per cent of households in the 'less than 24 kirat' class had ever purchased land, whereas the incidence is substantially higher for the other groups. Another way of measuring the impact of land sales on current land distribution would be to compare the proportion of land bought by each income class with their share in current land ownership. Here we see that 45 per cent of total area purchased went to those with large land ownerships (240-480 kirats) and that this is larger than this group's share of 16.5 per cent in current land ownership. In contrast to this, the 'less than 24 kirat' category accounted for only 4.5 per cent of total area purchased although it accounted for 17 per cent of current land ownership. Land purchases have thus contributed to a greater concentration of land ownership.

Broadly, the same picture is obtained when land loss and purchases are analysed according to their distribution by income class. Land was mainly lost by the poor and mainly acquired by the rich, and Tables 4.15 and 4.16 are self-explanatory on this point.

Table 4.15: Land Purchases by Income Class

Income Class (£E)	Total No. of Households	No. of Purchases	Total Amount Purchased (kirats)	% Distribution
Less than 50	21	—	—	—
50.0-74.9	25	—	—	—
75.0-99.9	34	2	10	0.4
100.0-149.9	71	1	48	1.8
150.0-199.9	96	2	20	0.7
200.0-249.9	96	3	72	2.7
250.0-299.9	93	1	11	0.4
300.0-349.9	68	3	74	2.8
350.0-399.9	64	1	8	0.3
400.0-499.9	97	5	128	4.8
500.0-599.9	60	6	153	5.7
600.0-799.9	70	9	734	27.3
800.0-999.9	32	6	249	9.3
1 000.0-1 399.9	21	3	291	10.8
1 400.0-2 000.0	14	4	756	28.2
More than 2 000.0	4	1	130	4.8
Total	866	47	2 684	100.0

Table 4.16:   Land Lost by Income Class

Income Class (£E)	Total Number of House-holds	Sale		Forfeiture		Total		% Distri-bution of Area Lost
		No.	Area	No.	Area	No.	Area	
Less than 50.0	21	1	2	—	—	1	2	0.5
50.0-74.9	25	1	6	—	—	1	6	1.5
75.0-99.9	34	1	4	1	18	2	22	5.6
100.0-149.9	71	1	12	1	12	2	24	6.1
150.0-199.9	96	1	8	1	12	2	20	5.1
200.0-249.9	96	—	—	—	—	—	—	—
250.0-299.9	93	4	164	1	5	5	169	42.8
300.0-349.9	68	1	6	—	—	1	6	1.5
350.0-399.9	64	2	9	1	1	3	10	2.5
400.0-499.9	97	3	46	1	6	4	52	13.2
500.0-599.9	60	2	8	—	1	2	9	2.0
600.0-799.9	70	2	6	1	2	3	8	2.0
800.0-999.9	32	3	26	1	2	4	28	7.1
1 000.0-1 399.9	21	—	—	1	14	1	14	3.5
1 400.0-2 000.0	14	—	—	1	2	1	2	0.5
More than 2 000.0	4	—	—	1	24	1	24	6.1
Total	866	22	297	11	99	33	396	100.0

The pattern of land movements that we have described is thus perfectly consistent with the expected pattern of decumulation by the poor and accumulation by the rich in an agrarian society characterised by private ownership of land and a high degree of concentration in land ownership.

Farm Production

In the preceding sections we have attempted to establish the influence that access to land has on the distribution of income without looking at all into questions of farm production. We shall therefore conclude this chapter by rectifying this omission.

Crop product accounts for 79 per cent of the gross value of farm output and the remainder is accounted for by livestock and livestock products. Of this total farm output, 27 per cent is used for own-consumption by farming households. Looking at the pattern of own-consumption by size of landholding (Table 4.17), we find the expected tendency for the proportion of farm output that is used for own-consumption to fall with rising farm sizes. What is striking, however, is that even for very small farms own-consumption does not, in general, account for more than 30 to 40 per cent of gross output. Farm production is thus commercialised and predominantly subsistence production does not exist.

Table 4.17: Aspects of Farm Production

Size of Landholding (kirats)	No. of Farms	% Value of Own-consumption ÷ Gross Value of Farm Output	% of Farms Using Hired Labour	% of Farms Using Machinery
Less than 3.0	5	70.0	0.0	40.0
3.0-5.9	33	43.5	30.3	36.0
6.0-11.9	55	38.2	25.5	52.7
12.0-17.9	26	39.7	30.8	61.5
18.0-23.9	47	34.4	48.2	68.1
24.0-29.9	28	31.3	46.4	60.7
30.0-35.9	41	34.5	51.2	75.6
36.0-41.9	15	43.1	33.3	60.0
42.0-47.9	43	30.1	67.4	74.4
48.0-59.9	30	27.4	66.7	60.0
60.0-71.9	40	29.5	72.5	80.0
72.0-95.9	29	21.8	75.9	55.2
96.0-119.9	10	19.5	80.1	70.0
120.0-191.9	12	14.2	83.3	75.0
192.0-480.0	11	18.7	81.8	81.8

The high level of commercialisation is also evident from the pattern of input use. Modern inputs such as fertilisers and pesticides are almost universally used and there are no sharp variations in the intensity in the use of such inputs across farm sizes. For instance, there is no statistically significant trend in the proportion of purchased to total value of inputs across the farm sizes and the proportion of fertiliser to total input costs was negatively related to farm size. The fitted equation is:

$$\log Y = 1.287 - 0.1051 \log X$$
$$(0.0258)$$
$$R^2 = 0.038$$
$$n = 419$$

where: Y = purchase of fertilisers/total costs
        X = size of landholding.

The only significant variation in the pattern of input use relates to the use of hired labour where the proportion of farms in each class using hired labour increases sharply with farm size (see Chapter 6, p. 147).

Although only 16 households in our sample own any mechanically powered farm equipment, the use of the services of such machinery is very much more widespread. In our sample 63 per cent of the farms have a positive entry for 'operating costs of machinery' which was defined to include the cost of hiring such machinery. Although the proportion of farms using machinery shows the expected increase with farm size, it is striking that at least one-third of farms in the minuscule category of less than a quarter of a feddan make use of machinery. For farms larger than this but smaller than 1 feddan the proportion rises to over 60 per cent. Taking only those households which do use machinery, we find that the proportion of 'operating costs of machinery' to total costs rises with farm size but the elasticity coefficient is very low and the fit is very poor. The estimated equation is:

$$\log Y = 3.038 + 0.0984 \log X$$
$$(0.0356)$$

$R^2 = 0.0275$
$n = 269$
where: Y = operating costs of machinery total costs
$\qquad\quad X$ = size of landholding.

These facts about the pattern of farm production suggest that the system of supervised co-operatives in Egypt has been successful in diffusing the use of modern inputs and farm machinery to even the smallest production units. From the point of view of income distribution and poverty, however, this pattern of production implies that the potential for bringing about a sharp increase in the productivity of small farms through the introduction of modern inputs has already been largely exploited.

To complete this glimpse of farm production we note that the relationship of farm productivity to farm size follows the inverse relationship that has been frequently observed. The fitted equation is as follows:

$$\log Y = 2.6517 - 0.2559 \log X$$
$$(0.0363)$$
$R^2 = 0.1075$
$N = 425$
where: Y = net farm output per kirat
$\qquad\quad X$ = size of landholding.

Cropping intensity is negatively related to farm size, as is the input of family labour. The fitted equation for the latter is:

$$\log Y = 4.016 - 0.5154 \log X$$
$$(0.0354)$$

$R^2 = 0.3637$
$n = 415$
where: Y = days worked on family farm/size of landholding
X = size of landholding.

Thus, in rural Egypt, as is often the case elsewhere in Third World agriculture, resources are used more intensively on small family farms. Therefore, the scope exists, in the sphere of farm production, to raise total output and reduce income inequality through further land redistribution.

5 Poverty, Consumption and Basic Needs

In the previous chapters we have examined the extent of inequality in the distribution of income and ownership of assets. An attempt was also made to identify the main determinants of such a pattern of inequality. We shall now focus on the phenomenon of absolute rural poverty.[1] Our objective will be to provide a quantitative estimate of the incidence of poverty, explore its major determinants and construct a profile of the poor in terms of some basic socio-economic characteristics.

The Nature and Extent of Rural Poverty

The estimate of the incidence of poverty involves two distinct operations: 'identification' (who are the poor?) and 'aggregation' (how much aggregate poverty do the poverty magnitudes of the poor taken together imply?).[2]

The idenitifcation of the poor is usually done by following the conventional method of establishing a poverty line as the break-even level of income at which the consumption level of an individual or a household is nutritionally adequate, and defining as poor all those persons and households which fall below that level. As we shall demonstrate later, this method was found inadequate on two counts. First, the definition of a poverty line in terms of nutritional adequacy alone is not sufficient, especially in situations where extreme malnutrition is not prevalent. Here, a broader definition of the poverty line going beyond nutritional adequacy to include other attributes of poverty may be necessary. Secondly, the 'head count' method of defining as poor the proportion of the total population that happens to fall below a specified poverty line, irrespective of their distance from that line, does not distinguish between the degree of relative deprivation of various poverty groups and is, therefore, completely insensitive to the distribution of income among the poor. An attempt will be made to remedy this shortcoming by introducing alternative measures of poverty where estimates of absolute deprivation are supplemented by measures of relative deprivation.

The Definition of the Poverty Line

The starting point in the identification exercise was to establish the poverty line, bearing in mind the specific characteristics of our sample. The first step involved the calculation of the poverty line income (PLY), i.e. that level of income (per capita or per household) at which a certain minimal living standard (in terms of nutrition level, clothing, housing, etc.) is most likely to be achieved given the prevailing income distribution pattern, price relationships, consumer preferences and cultural norms. An attempt was made to calculate the PLY on the basis of the observed income elasticity of calorie intake per household and per capita. This required, first, the conversion of the food basket of each household in the sample into calorie equivalents using a modified version of the FAO/WHO conversion tables.[3] Then we worked out the nutritional requirements of an adult equivalent unit (AEU) based on the age and sex structure and, as an indicator of energy expenditure, the employment characteristics of the sample population.[4] The calorie requirements of this reference AEU amounted to 2,545 calories per day, which is very close to the FAO's estimate of 2,510 per day.[5] Finally, we tried to work out the PLY, i.e. that household income and that per capita (defined as AEU) income at which we should expect the minimum calorie requirements to be satisfied. Various formulae were used to calculate the PLY on the basis of the observed income elasticity of calorie intake using both grouped and ungrouped data, for household and per capita distributions and using income and expenditure figures. Although figures gave a better fit while using grouped rather than ungrouped data, and expenditure rather than income, none of the formulae used gave meaningful results. The following examples demonstrate the point:

Regression Analysis of Determinants of Calorie Intake

a. Dependent variable: calorie intake per capita

Explanatory variables	Regression coefficient	Standard error	R^2
1. Household income	0.217	0.0099	0.0472
2. Per capita income	0.523	0.0113	0.2734

b. Dependent variable: calorie intake per household

Explanatory variables	Regression coefficient	Standard error	R^2	R^2 change
1. Household size	0.754	0.015	0.8505	0.8505
2. Household income	0.259	0.011	0.8890	0.0385

Moreover, solving the second formula for PLY needed to guarantee the minimum calorie intake for a household of five adult equivalents gives the figure of £E54 per year, which is unrealistically low if compared with £E270 for 1974/5.[6] The significance of this result is very clear: differences in household incomes are not sufficient to explain the variations in calorie intake. This is reflected in the formula where household size assumes an important role in 'explaining' variations in calorie intake while income 'explains' less than 4 per cent of this variation (see R^2 change).

The preceding results have some extremely important implications for the methodology of poverty measurement: estimating the PLY on the basis of the relationship between income and calorie intake alone is not sufficient. This is particularly true in cases where extreme destitution is not prevalent. In Egypt's case, this may be particularly true. Of our sample of 867 households, only 10 could be described as extremely destitute in the sense that their calorie intake fell below the 1,557 calories per capita per day prescribed by the FAO as the 'critical limit'.[7]

In view of the above an alternative method was used to define the poverty line. According to this approach the poverty line income was calculated, independently, in two stages. First, an estimate was made of the value of the food component of the PLY, i.e. the cost of the diet which fulfils the minimum nutritional requirements of the reference adult equivalent unit of our sample of 2,545 calories per day. The composition of the food basket that made up such a diet was obtained by reference to the observed consumption pattern of that income group whose annual income ranged from £E250–300, this being the range where the median income for the whole sample falls. The choice of the income group around the median income of the sample as the cut-off point was based on two considerations: (a) that this was the best approximation of the poverty group at the margin; and (b) that at this income level the Engle's ratio (ratio of expenditure on food to total expenditure) falls noticeably. A list was thus obtained containing quantities of the various types of foods that can satisfy the specified energy requirement and that are usually consumed by the poorer groups (Table 5.1). The cost of this diet was calculated by multiplying the quantities of the various types of food which appear on the list by the unit price prevailing in the market during the reference period (January 1977) and actually paid by this income group. As can be seen from Table 5.1, the value of a minimum diet per capita amounted to £E40 in 1977.

Table 5.1: Value of Diet Satisfying Minimum Calorie Requirements in Rural Egypt (all figures on per capita basis)

Item	Quantities		Value		Calorie Content
	Per Day (kg)	Per Year (kg)	Per Day (£E)	Per Year (£E)	Per Day
Wheat	0.1128	41.2	0.0066	2.409	395
Maize	0.1110	40.5	0.0062	2.263	400
Millet	0.0035	1.3	0.0002	0.073	12
Flour	0.1476	53.8	0.0062	2.263	546
Rice	0.0613	27.4	0.0047	1.715	220
Others – macaroni	0.1790	65.3	0.0020	0.730	90
Beans	0.0196	7.2	0.0018	0.657	68
Lentils	0.0138	5.0	0.0028	1.022	47
Fenugreek	0.0048	1.8	0.0007	0.256	17
Other pulses	0.0046	1.7	0.0009	0.339	31
Meat	0.0181	6.6	0.0259	9.454	40
Poultry	0.0040	1.5	0.0033	1.205	9
Fish – fresh	0.0074	2.7	0.0027	0.986	10
Fish – canned	0.0002	0.1	0.0002	0.073	1
Eggs	0.0111	4.1	0.0031	1.132	18
Oil	0.0107	3.9	0.0028	1.022	99
Fat	0.0102	3.7	0.0027	0.986	90
Milk	0.0112	4.1	0.0013	0.475	11
Cheese	0.0272	9.9	0.0038	1.387	27
Ghee	0.0050	1.8	0.0065	2.373	47
Potatoes	0.0400	14.6	0.0037	1.351	33
Onions	0.0263	9.6	0.0020	0.730	11
Tomatoes	0.0452	16.5	0.0044	1.606	18
Other vegetables	0.0205	7.5	0.0014	0.511	8
Citrons	0.0433	15.8	0.0026	0.949	12
Dates	0.0006	0.2	0.0001	0.037	1
Other fruits	0.0006	0.2	0.0001	0.037	1
Sugar	0.0457	16.7	0.0071	2.592	177
Sugar products	0.0030	1.1	0.0006	0.219	8
Cooked beans	—	—	0.0013	0.475	44
Falafel	—	—	0.0016	0.584	54
Total	0.9883	365.8	0.1093	39.911	2 545

Note: To obtain the market value of the diet which satisfies minimum calorie requirements the following steps were followed: (1) the quantities, values and calorie content of the diet actually consumed by the median income group were worked out from the consumption tables; (2) in view of the discrepancy between the calorie content of this group's diet (2,864 calories per capita per day) and the minimum required diet (2,545 calories per capita per day), the former was scaled down proportionately to get the quantities of the various food items that would produce 2,545 calories and that were likely to be consumed by the median income group; (3) the cost of items thus obtained was calculated by multiplying their quantities by the unit prices actually paid by the median income group; and the total cost of the minimum diet was obtained as the sum of the cost of these items.

The second stage in calculating the PLY was to estimate the value of the non-food component which is associated with these minimum nutritional requirements. This estimate was based on the ratio of expenditure on food to total expenditure of that group of households whose actual spending on food is nearest to the value of the minimum diet. This was the income group of £E250-300 and the food/total expenditure ratio amounted to 60 per cent. On the basis of this ratio the value of the non-food component was calculated and added to the value of the minimum diet. The total represents the value of per capita income necessary to ensure a minimum nutritional and basic consumption level, or the poverty-line income.[8] This amounted to £E67 at 1977 prices.[9]

It is customary that once the poverty line is established, the magnitude of poverty is measured by defining as poor all those households that fall below that line. The underlying assumption here is that the household would satisfy its minimum needs once it had command over the poverty line income. But evidence suggests that it may not necessarily be right to assume optimal consumer behaviour. There is no guarantee that every household in a given income group would have a consumption pattern that coincides with the composition of the basket of goods that satisfies those needs. This is not unique in Egypt. In fact, the pioneer of poverty studies, S. Rowntree, distinguished between primary and secondary poverty. *Primary poverty* was insufficient income to buy minimum needs while *secondary poverty* was the case when people had more than adequate income but did not spend it on satisfying their minimum physiological needs.[10]

Thus, if we define poverty in terms of the PLY alone we shall find that out of our sample of 867 households, 486 (56 per cent of households and 61 per cent of population) fell below the poverty line and on this criterion would be classified as poor, while 381 (44 per cent of households and 39 per cent of population) were above the poverty line and thus would be considered as non-poor. If we take a broader view of poverty by looking at its other attributes, a much more complex picture will emerge. For instance, we shall find that among the group of households falling below the poverty-line income, there are those whose members suffer from calorie deficiency and those who satisfy their nutritional requirements. The same observation is true for the non-poor group.

In view of the inadequacy of the income criterion in defining poverty, we have decided to extend our definition to include nutritional adequacy besides income availability. Thus our definition of poverty will be based on two criteria:

(i)   inadequacy of income in the sense that household income falls
      below the PLY estimated earlier as equal to an annual expenditure
      of £E67 per capita; *plus*
(ii) nutritional deficiency, i.e. the shortfall in calorie intake from
      calorie requirement. The estimate of the shortfall (or surplus) of
      calorie intake for each household was based on a comparison of
      the observed calorie content of the food basket that may have
      been consumed by each household member with that particular
      member's energy requirements given his age, sex and the effort
      required for the type of work he performs. Estimates of
      consumption and requirements were converted to adult equivalent
      units assuming equality in intra-family distribution of consumption.

Table 5.2 sums up the results of applying this definition of poverty.
On the basis of the two criteria proposed above, we can distinguish
between four sub-groups of households:

(i)   306 households which may be described as *definitely poor* as
      their income per capita falls below the PLY and their calorie
      intake falls short of their energy requirements (Rowntree's
      'primary poverty' group);
(ii) 180 households which can be described as *marginal* in view of
      the fact that while they satisfy their nutritional requirements, their
      incomes fall short of PLY;
(iii) 281 households qualify for the term *non-poor* on both counts;
      and
(iv) 100 households which despite some calorie deficiency have
      incomes higher than the PLY, and would therefore be
      considered as *non-poor*. This group is similar to Rowntree's
      'secondary poverty' group where the household's 'total earnings
      would be sufficient for the maintenance of merely physical
      efficiency were it not that some portion of it is absorbed by other
      expenditure, either useful or wasteful'.[11]

The above picture is much more complex and perhaps more
realistic than that provided by the conventional poverty measures.
Here, there is no unique cut-off point that separates the poor from the
non-poor, but rather a spectrum with households that are unambiguously poor (group (i)) or non-poor (group (iii)) at either end and,

Table 5.2: The Poor and the Non-poor in Rural Egypt

		Households		Household Members		Adult Equivalent Units (AEU)		Household Size
		No.	%	No.	%	No.	%	
(i)	Primary poverty: definitely poor	306	35.3	2 172	42.3	1 772	41.5	7.1
(ii)	Marginal: low income but calorie surplus	180	20.8	957	18.6	814	19.1	5.3
(iii)	Definitely non-poor	281	32.4	1 345	26.2	1 138	26.7	4.8
(iv)	Secondary poverty: higher income but calorie deficient	100	11.5	662	12.9	542	12.7	6.6
	Total/average	867	100.0	5 136	100.0	4 266	100.0	5.9

Table 5.2: The Poor and the Non-poor in Rural Egypt (contd)

		Calorie per AEU per Day			Protein Intake	Annual Income (£E)		Total Expenditure (£E)	
		Requirements	Intake	% +/-[a]	Per AEU	Household	AEU	Household	AEU
(i)	Primary poverty: definitely poor	2 914	2 332	-20	57.4	327.0	56.9	278.6	47.6
(ii)	Marginal: low income but calorie surplus	2 526	2 946	+17	74.0	267.0	57.0	244.6	53.4
(iii)	Definitely non-poor	2 648	3 462	+31	84.0	461.7	121.1	440.6	115.0
(iv)	Secondary poverty: higher income but calorie deficient	3 107	2 642	-15	63.7	553.7	109.3	496.1	92.4
	Total/average	2 793	2 861	+2.4	68.5	383.8	83.8	349.1	75.8

Note a: (Intake- Requirements) ÷ (Requirements).

in between, households whose position is not as clearly defined (groups (ii) and (iv)).

We shall, however, define as poor all households in groups (i) and (ii) and the rest as non-poor. This definition, while as arbitrary as any other definition of poverty, was based on a careful examination of the household characteristics in each group. The position of groups (i) – the primary poverty group – and (iii) – the definitely non-poor – needs no explanation and, as we shall see later, will be confirmed with our study of other attributes of poverty. It is, however, the positions of groups (ii) – the marginally poor – and (iv) – the secondary poverty group – that need some clarification. The inclusion of group (ii) in the 'poor' category was based on the fact that it had all the attributes of poverty except calorie deficiency. As Table 5.2 shows, this group was spending almost all (92 per cent) of its income on consumption. Moreover, a high proportion of expenditure (66.5 per cent) was spent on food. More important perhaps, the greater part of their calorie requirements (1,900 out of 2,526 calories per person per day or 75 per cent) was generated from cereals, whose prices are relatively lower than other sources of energy. This is a familiar case where the poor try to satisfy their nutritional requirements through the consumption of 'inferior goods', i.e. food items with cheaper cost per unit of calorie. It should also be emphasised that the position of this group remains vulnerable and its members are the most likely candidates to join the ranks of the poor in case, for instance, of a sudden rise in the price of cereals.

The position of group (iv), where households command income higher than the PLY but appear to have a slight nutritional deficiency, can also be explained by reference to their consumption behaviour. A detailed analysis of that group's expenditure pattern shows that:

(i)   expenditure on non-food items, especially clothing, transport and education, is relatively more important than in the case of other groups; and

(ii) they favour 'superior goods' in their diets which is evidenced by a high proportion of their expenditure on food (between 30 and 40 per cent) being spent on meat.

It appears, therefore, that the consumption behaviour of that group bears the characteristics of the non-poor. The fact that the households show a shortfall in calorie intake can be explained by their preference for 'superior goods' such as meat, which are lower in calorie content but higher in other nutrients such as protein, a fact reflected in their relatively high protein intake (Table 5.2).

The Incidence of Poverty

Having established the definition of poverty in the context of rural Egypt, we shall now turn to the measurement of its incidence. Two standard indices have hitherto been used to measure the extent of poverty: the 'head count' and the 'poverty gap'. The *head count index* (widely used in the quantification of poverty, since Booth and Rowntree still provide the basis for poverty statistics and anti-poverty programmes) is given by the proportion of the total population that happens to fall below the poverty line. According to this measure, we find that in 1977 some 35 per cent of rural households in Egypt, comprising 42 per cent of the rural population, were living in poverty. The other measure of poverty is the *poverty gap index*, which is the total income needed to bring all the poor up to the poverty line. This index is usually expressed as the percentage shortfall of the average income of the poor from the poverty line, or the income-gap ratio.[12] In the case of rural Egypt, the *average* poverty gap would amount to £E19.40 per person per year, or 29 per cent of the poverty-line income.

Both measures have serious limitations that may drastically reduce their usefulness.[13] The head count index may provide a rough indicator of the magnitude of the poverty problem, but it is obviously a very crude one as it ignores the amounts by which incomes of the poor fall short of the poverty line. Thus, 'an unchanged number of the people below the poverty line may go with a sharp rise in the extent of the shortfall of income from the poverty line'.[14] Moreover, this measure is completely insensitive to the distribution of income among the poor. Consequently, a transfer of income from a poor person to one who is richer can never increase the poverty measure since the poor person from whom the transfer takes place is, in any case, counted as poor, and no reduction of his income will make him count any more than he does already.[15] The poverty gap index, like the head count measure, is insensitive to the distribution of income among the poor. Moreover, unlike the head count measure, the poverty gap index pays no attention whatsoever to the number or proportion of poor people below the poverty line, concentrating only on the aggregate shortfall, no matter how it is distributed and among how many.

To illustrate the limitations of these measures, we shall present in Table 5.3 the extent of the shortfall of per capita expenditure from the established poverty line of £E67 for the households in primary poverty distributed by the shortfall in their calorie intake as one indicator of the

Table 5.3:   Income Shortfall from the Poverty Line for Different Poverty Groups

Calorie Shortfall as % of Requirements[a]	Expenditure per Year[b] (£E)	Income Gap per Capita[c] (£E)	As % of PLY	No. of Households	% Total
Less than 5.0	55.1	11.9	17.8	35	11.4
5.0-9.9	51.9	15.1	22.5	47	15.4
10.0-14.9	48.4	18.6	27.8	46	15.0
15.0-19.9	52.3	14.7	21.9	31	10.1
20.0-24.9	47.4	19.6	29.3	53	19.3
25.0-29.9	46.9	20.1	30.0	32	10.5
30.0-39.9	39.5	27.5	41.0	43	14.1
40.0-50.0	34.4	32.6	48.7	14	4.6
More than 50.0	31.1	35.9	53.6	5	1.6
Average	47.6	19.4	28.7		

Notes: a. Shortfall of calorie intake per adult equivalent unit from requirements.
b. Mean expenditure per adult equivalent unit.
c. Shortfall of per capita from the poverty line of £E67 as % of the latter.
In view of these serious shortcomings, we have decided to supplement the standard measures of poverty with a new one proposed by A.K. Sen (see note 15). Sen's proposed measure incorporates in a single index the three concerns lacking in the standard measures: sensitivity to the absolute number of people in poverty; sensitivity to transfers among and within income groups; and sensitivity to income distribution among the poor.

degree of their deprivation. It is evident that the standard measure ignores important differences among the poverty groups in terms of the relative distance from the poverty line. As we can see from the table, these distances vary widely (ranging from about 18 per cent to 54 per cent of the poverty line), and the poor population is not evenly distributed below the poverty line. To talk in terms of averages or to pay no attention to the differences among the poverty groups can, therefore, be misleading.

Sen's index provides a measure of poverty in terms of the income needed to support all the population in poverty at the poverty-line level. This index differs from the standard measure in at least two major respects: (a) the measure of poverty should be concerned not merely with the number of people below the poverty line but also with amounts by which the incomes of the poor fall short of the specified poverty level; and (b) the bigger the shortfall from the poverty levels, the greater should be the weight per unit of that shortfall in the poverty measure.[16]

Thus, the Sen index is axiomatically derived assuming the poverty measure to be a 'normalised weighted sum of the income gaps of the poor'. Two axioms then suffice to derive the index: the first specifies the income weighting scheme, and the second stipulates the normalisation procedure. Sen chooses the rank-order weighting scheme, in which the income gap of a poor person is simply his rank in the income ordering below the poverty line. Sen's normalisation axiom requires that when all the poor have the same income, the index takes a value equal to the proportion of persons in poverty multiplied by the proportionate average shortfall of their income from the poverty line. Sen's index can be formally presented as follows:

$$P = \frac{q}{n} \cdot \frac{1}{z} \; [z - m(1 - G)]$$

where: n = total population size
z = poverty line
q = number of people in poverty (i.e. with income less than or equal to z)
m = mean income of the poor
G = Gini coefficient of the distribution of income among the poor.

The relationship with the standard measures of poverty is immediately clear: the head count index is given by q/n, the average poverty gap is given by $(z - m)$ and the proportionate income shortfall from the poverty line would be equal to

$$\frac{z - m}{z} \, .$$

Furthermore, the Sen index can be modified to measure the percentage of GNP needed to close the poverty gap. This index will be:

$$M = \frac{q}{n} \cdot \frac{1}{u} \; [z - m(1 - G)]$$

and its relationship to P is given by:

$$M = \frac{z}{u} \cdot P$$

where: u = mean income of population.

Estimates of Sen's index using our data are presented, together with the standard measures of poverty, in Table 5.4. As mentioned earlier, the percentage of the rural population in poverty in Egypt was calculated as 42 per cent, and the average poverty gap as £E19.40 per person per year. The poverty gap as a fraction of the total income needed to support everyone in the poor population at the poverty level (Sen's P index) amounts to 11.3 per cent (or £E7.57). It is, therefore, clear that using Sen's index gives a lower estimate of the resources needed for the alleviation of poverty. The M index was estimated at 0.100, which implies that the poverty gap in rural Egypt stands at 10 per cent of the total personal income of the rural population (or £E7.580).

Table 5.4: Estimates of Poverty in Rural Egypt

Proportion of Persons in Poverty $(q/n)^a$	Average Poverty Gap (z/m) in £E per Capita per Year[b]	Weighted Poverty Gap ('Sen's Index'[c])		Gini Coefficient of Income Distribution among the Poor
		P	*M*	
0.415	19.4	0.113	0.100	0.069

Notes: a. Number of adult equivalent units in households below the poverty line as percentage of total AEU.
b. £E67.00 − 47.60.
The various measures presented above describe different aspects of the poverty problem. The head count index provides an estimate of the *incidence* of poverty in terms of the number of population in poverty, thus enabling us to identify the magnitude of the problem or the size of the 'target group'. The poverty gap estimates provide an indicator of the income shortfall of the poor, which is an important indicator of the *extent* of poverty and a useful guide in calculating the cost of anti-poverty programmes.

Profile of Poverty in Rural Egypt

So far we have been concerned with the measurement of the incidence of poverty. In an attempt to provide a diagnosis of the nature and causes of poverty in rural Egypt, we shall now draw on the results of the survey to present a 'profile' of the poor households in terms of some of the major socio-economic variables. We shall distinguish between two sets of these variables: one which includes some of the major attributes of poverty such as food intake, consumption pattern and access to basic needs which we shall call the characteristics of poverty; and the other, which we shall call the sources or causes of poverty, includes such variables as employment, income generation, asset ownership and demographic factors.[17] It should be emphasised, however, that this distinction between the 'characteristics' and 'causes' of poverty is introduced only to facilitate analysis and should not imply any categorical divorce between these two sets of variables. Employment status can be considered as much a characteristic of poverty as a causative variable that explains the source of poverty.

Since the household is the basic income sharing unit, it would appear more appropriate (especially for policy purposes) for the analysis of the nature and causes of poverty to be done in terms of the household, rather than individual characteristics of the poor population.

The Characteristics of Poverty

In this section we shall examine some of the manifestations of poverty in three broad areas: nutrition, consumption of non-food goods and access to some basic needs (education and housing). This will be done not only by drawing on the data relating to the poor, as defined in this study, but also by contrasting these to the rest of the rural population.

(a) Nutritional adequacy. Nutritional adequacy is the most widely used indicator of poverty. An individual or a household may be considered poor if the nutritive value of his diet (usually expressed in terms of calories) falls short of his requirements. It is a common practice to measure the extent of poverty by the shortfall of calorie intake from the requirements of a 'reference man'.[18] In the present study, we have rejected this method in favour of another which measures the calorie gap in terms of the shortfall of calorie intake of a certain household from the requirements of its members given their age, sex and the type of effort they perform. The results were presented in Table 5.2, from which it appears that the 42 per cent of population in poverty suffer from a calorie shortfall of 20 per cent of the amount required to renew their energy every day. By contrast, the 'definitely non-poor' group enjoyed a surplus of 31 per cent of their own requirements.

To estimate the calorie gap more accurately, we should go beyond those averages. Table 5.5 and Figure 5.1 present a detailed picture of the calorie shortfall for the various poverty groups. A number of points emerge here. *First*, an insignificant proportion of the poor can be described as seriously undernourished, since their calorie intake was below the FAO minimum 'critical limit' of 1,557 calories per person per day. As we mentioned earlier, only 10 households out of 868 fell in that category. *Secondly*, the bottom 20 per cent of the poor population

Table 5.5: The Calorie Gap of the Poor Population

Calorie Deficit as % of Requirements	Average Annual Expenditure (£E)	Calorie Requirements per Capita per Day	Calorie Intake per Capita per Day	Difference as % of Requirements	No. of Households	% to Total
Less than 5.0	55.1	2 841	2 762	2.8	35	11.4
5.0-9.9	51.9	2 836	2 626	7.4	47	15.4
10.0-14.9	48.4	2 818	2 461	12.7	46	15.0
15.0-19.9	52.3	2 964	2 454	17.2	31	10.1
20.0-24.9	47.4	2 918	2 256	22.7	53	17.3
25.0-29.9	46.9	3 074	2 231	27.4	32	10.5
30.0-39.9	39.5	3 016	1 973	34.6	43	14.1
40.0-50.0	34.4	2 920	1 626	44.3	14	4.6
More than 50.0	31.1	2 782	1 149	58.7	5	1.6
Averages/totals	47.6	2 914	2 332	20.0	306	100.0

Figure 5.1:   The Calorie Gap of the Poor Population

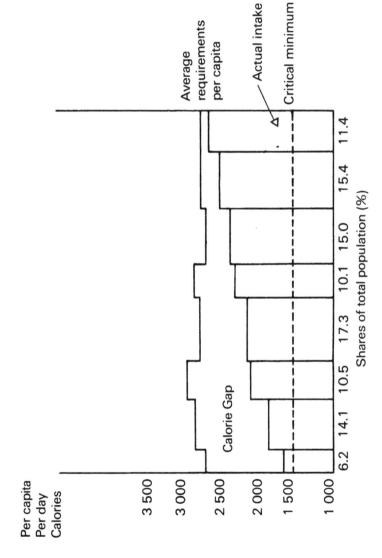

appear to have nutrition problem, as they suffer from a calorie deficit of some 35 per cent or more of their requirements, while the upper 40 per cent have a deficit that does not exceed 13 per cent of their requirements. *Thirdly,* there seems to be an almost direct relationship between calorie deficit and calorie intake requirements, i.e. those with the highest deficit are those with the highest requirements and vice versa, indicating that the poorer sections of the population may be engaged in the types of heavy activities that require higher energy inputs. This last point illustrates the inadequacy of the traditional measures of poverty which define the calorie gap as the difference between actual intake and some average requirement of the population as a whole, making no distinction whatever between the different requirements of different people, thus giving an unrealistic assessment of the extent of undernourishment of the various poverty groups.

Poor households appear to suffer from protein deficiency as well as calorie inadequacy. Table 5.2 showed that the protein intake of the poor amounted to 57.4 grams per person per day. This represents some 76.6 per cent of the safe level of 75.0 grams per person per day recommended by the FAO,[19] and comes to only 68.3 per cent of the daily protein intake of the non-poor which was 84.0 grams per person. This is not a surprising finding. It goes to support the view now widely held that the diets of the poor which are protein-deficient are also calorie-deficient.[20] It is not our intention to dismiss the problem of protein deficiency of the poor, but rather to point to an important policy implication of the above observation; namely that an increase in dietary intake to adequate calorie levels, even assuming no major change in the diet pattern, would also lead to adequacy in protein intake. It should, however, be emphasised that an adequate calorie intake, while ensuring the renewal of a person's energy, does not compensate for a certain minimum of protein intake which is necessary as a preventive nutrient without which the body may be vulnerable to disease.

The nutritional status of the poor can be explained by reference to their dietary pattern. Table 5.6 provides a summary view of the relative shares of different food items in the consumption expenditure of various income groups. One feature that emerges from this table is that the diet of the poor is largely *cereal-based* while that of the non-poor is much more diversified. We note that the poor households spend one-third of their food budget on cereals and one-quarter on meat (which may have been over-reported). It is almost the reverse for the non-poor with one-third of their food budget spent on meat and only 26 per cent on cereals. A corollary of this situation is that the poor derive more than 65 cent of their

Table 5.6:   Percentage Expenditure on Food Items Relative to Household Total Expenditure, 1977 (survey)

	Poor and Marginal Households	Non-poor Households	Total Households
Total household expenditure (£E)	266.0	455.0	349.0
% expenditure on food and beverages	68.2	56.6	63.1
Cereals and starches	24.0	14.6	19.8
Meat, fish and eggs	16.3	17.5	16.8
Milk and dairy products	5.7	6.6	6.1
Vegetables	6.4	5.3	5.9
Fruits	1.0	1.5	1.2

Table 5.7:   Percentage Expenditure on Food Items Relative to Household Total Expenditure, 1958/9 and 1964/5   (Egypt)

	1958/9	1964/5
Total household expenditure (£E)	148.0	224.0
% expenditure on food and beverages	64.3	64.4
Cereals and starches	26.8	24.5
Meat, fish and eggs	11.0	14.0
Milk and dairy products	8.1	7.6
Vegetables	3.3	4.1
Fruits	2.0	1.9

Source: Family Budget Surveys.

calorie intake from cereals and starches while 'superior goods' such as meat, fish, eggs and dairy products (which are also major sources of protein contribute no more than 6.3 per cent of the total calorie intake. Table 5.7, which compares our results with previous surveys, shows that this dietary pattern has not changed over the last twenty years.

The prominence of cereals and starches in the diet of the poor can be explained by their relatively low price-calorie terms in the sense that the proportion of calorie intake from these foods is particularly high in relation to their prices. To support this argument, we shall present in Table 5.8 the comparative price-calorie terms for the major food commodities showing the money cost a person would have to pay for 100 calories' worth of these commodities given the prevailing pattern of relative prices. It is immediately clear that the consumption behaviour of the poor is 'perfectly rational' as they demand the commodities which have a lower cost per unit of calorie. In fact, they can do nothing else. The degree of substitution between different foods seems to be extremely limited given the relative price relationships. It is difficult for a poor household to substitute beans, which cost 2.6 milliems per 100 calories, with meat, which costs 25 times as much. That is to say, given the pattern of relative prices a poor family has to pay for food, there is a very limited and rigid number of combinations that will yield, approximately the same calorific value, given the family's low income.[21] This situation has some important policy implications: any poverty redressal policy should aim at lowering the price-calorie terms for those food commodities that are considered major sources of energy and protein and *under no circumstances* allow the relative price of the basic commodities (cereals) to rise, as this may threaten the main source of energy for the poor. In Egypt, the price policies of the 1950s and 1960s aimed exactly at this objective and, as Table 5.8 shows, the relative prices of cereals and pulses remained quite stable. This trend seems to have been slowly reversed since the early 1970s. The rapid increase in real incomes may only result in the poor's inability to satisfy their calorie inake, thus making a bad situation worse.

Table 5.8: Relative Cost of a 100 Calorie Equivalent of Some Food Commodities

Commodity	Price (milliems)	% of Maize = 100
Wheat	1.8	113
Maize	1.6	100
Rice	2.1	131
Beans	2.6	163
Lentils	5.6	350
Meat	64.8	4 050
Poultry	64.8	4 050
Fish	27.0	1 688
Eggs	17.2	1 075
Milk	11.8	738
Cheese	14.1	881
Potatoes	11.2	700
Tomatoes	24.4	1 525
Onions	18.2	1 138
Vegetables	17.5	1 094
Citrons	21.7	1 356
Other fruits	10.0	625

(b) The consumption pattern. The consumption pattern of the poor in rural Egypt is typical of many Third World countries with food accounting for over 63 per cent of total expenditure, followed by

clothing, 8 per cent; fuel and light, 3.2 per cent; rent, 1.5 per cent. Basic services account for only a fraction of expenditure: education, 0.8 per cent; medical care, 2.0 per cent. At the end of the list comes expenditure on consumer durables, the share of which is negligible, 0.6 per cent. By contrast, the non-poor spend just over half (53 per cent) of their expenditure on food, leaving more to spend on other goods, especially basic services, with the share of education amounting to 1.3 per cent, and medical care to 3.1 per cent (Table 5.9).

Table 5.9: Consumption Patterns: Percentage Distribution of Consumption Expenditure

Consumption Items	Poor and Marginal Households	Non-poor Households	Total Households
Food	63.4	53.3	58.9
Beverages	4.8	3.3	4.2
Stimulants	5.8	8.1	6.8
Fuel and light	3.2	3.1	3.1
Domestic and personal	1.4	1.4	1.4
Total consumer goods	78.6	69.2	74.4
Rent	1.5	3.1	2.2
Transport	6.8	8.4	7.5
Clothing	7.7	7.9	7.8
Consumer durables	0.6	1.4	1.0
Medical care	2.0	3.1	2.5
Education	0.8	1.3	1.0
Transfer payments	0.9	3.3	2.0
Others	1.2	2.4	1.6
Total expenditure	100.0	100.0	100.0

A comparison of this pattern of consumption with those revealed by the three Household Budget Surveys suggests that the composition of the consumption basket of the rural poor has remained more or less unchanged over the last two decades. Expenditure on food has always dominated the family budget with its share in total consumption decreasing only slightly from 64 per cent in 1958/9 to about 62 per cent in 1977.

We were unable to establish the extent to which the consumption of the non-food items by the poor falls short of their basic needs in the absence of any information on the norms for the minimum requirements of the rural population for such goods as clothing, education and medical care. We can safely assume, however, that the fact that income per capita of the poor households falls below the poverty-line income (which is equal to the level of income at which these needs are supposed to be met) implies that at least some of the basic needs of the poor would go unsatisfied under the prevailing income distribution pattern and relative price structure. The following discussion on the educational status and housing structures of the poor will no doubt support this argument.

(c) Access to basic needs. To complete our outline of the characteristics of poverty, we shall now examine the access, or rather the lack of access, of the rural poor to two basic services: housing and education.

Housing: Table 5.10 provides some selected indicators of the housing conditions for various income groups in rural Egypt. The picture that emerges is one of poor housing conditions for the rural population as a whole: the majority of the houses (79 per cent) are built of 'green', or mud-bricks, and are terribly lacking in facilities; only 19 per cent have potable water, 23 per cent have electric light and 43 per cent are provided with a toilet of some kind. This picture is consistent with conditions in the countryside as a whole. The 1976 Population Census reports that out of the 3.7 million households of rural Egypt only 14 per cent had piped water in their houses, 36 per cent had no access to clean drinking water whatever, and the remaining 50 per cent of the population depended on water supply from a communal point in the village.[22] The Census also shows that only 18.6 per cent of the households had electric light.[23] The contrast with the urban areas is striking. Out of the 3.2 million households in urban Egypt, about 70 per cent lived in houses with piped water and 77 per cent had electric light.[24]

This general picture should not overshadow the important differences in housing conditions of the various income groups. As Table 5.10 shows, the overwhelming majority of the poor and marginal households (87 per cent and 84 per cent respectively) live in mud-brick houses, some 3-7 per cent in huts and only 8-10 per cent live in red-brick houses. Moreover, the houses of the poor households are extremely poor in facilities: only 16 per cent have drinking water, 12 per cent electricity and 30 per cent have toilets. Another aspect of the poor housing conditions is reflected by the relatively high room density for the poor households: 2.5 persons per room compared to 1.5 for the non-poor.[25]

An interesting aspect of the housing situation in rural Egypt is that the majority of the families (86 per cent) own their houses. This has been one of the major features of the social history of the Egyptian

Table 5.10: Housing Conditions in Rural Egypt

| Household Groups | Owner-occupied Houses by Type of Building | | | | | | | | | | |
| | Red-brick | | | Mud-brick | | | Hut | | | Total | |
	No.	%	Average Value (£E)	No.	%	Average Value (£E)	No.	%	Average Value (£E)	No.	%
Poor	27	10.0	749	235	87.0	198	8	3.0	40	270	100
Marginal	13	8.8	904	124	84.4	183	10	6.8	21	147	100
Non-poor	99	30.0	1 177	232	70.0	354	—	—	—	331	100
Totals/averages	139	18.6	1 068	591	79.0	250	18	2.4	29	748	100

Table 5.10: Housing Conditions in Rural Egypt (contd.)

| Household Groups | Facilities | | | | | | Density | |
| | Potable Water | | Electricity | | Toilets | | Average Rooms per House | Average Persons per Room |
	No.	%	No.	%	No.	%		
Poor households	49	16	37	12	94	30	3.1	2.5
Marginal households	30	17	21	12	46	26	2.9	1.9
Non-poor households	88	23	139	36	230	60	3.8	1.5
Totals/averages	167	19	197	23	370	43	3.4	2.0

village where the family is defined by the house they must own, however modest this house may be.[26] A combination of rapid population growth and extreme scarcity of building land has reinforced the tradition of the extended family with the result that many houses are now overcrowded. It should be emphasised, however, that living in rented houses (or rooms), which was hardly known in Egyptian villages until the 1960s, is now becoming more and more common. Of our sample, 14 per cent of the families lived in rented dwellings. This must represent an added burden on the poor by drawing on their meagre incomes. The 12 per cent of poor families that lived in rented dwellings had to pay an average 7 per cent of their total expenditure for rent.

Education: The distribution of population by type of schooling completed is used here as a rough indicator of access to educational services.[27] It appears from Table 5.11 that an overwhelming majority of the rural population (92.5 per cent) have not completed their primary educaton. This category can be regarded as largely illiterate or semi-illiterate. It is unfortunate that we did not try to collect information on functional literacy, but we can safely assume that at least 70 per cent of the adult population (over 10 years of age) are illiterate. The 1976 Census, for instance, reported an adult literacy rate of 40 per cent for the country as a whole.[28]

The differentiation between the poor and the non-poor is also apparent here: while the proportion of people with less than primary education amounted to 95.4 per cent of the poor, the ratio falls to 87.6 per cent in the case of the non-poor. More important perhaps is that relatively higher proportion of the non-poor population was able to complete various types of schooling. We find that 4.8 per cent completed primary schooling, 3.1 per cent completed preparatory, 43.7 per cent completed secondary and 0.3 per cent completed higher education. On the other hand, 2.9 per cent of the poor population have completed their primary education, 1.7 per cent their preparatory and secondary, and only one person his higher education.

We collected no systematic information on the availability of educational and cultural facilities in the villages surveyed. However, historical evidence, confirmed by our observation, indicates that the Egyptian village has been grossly deprived of such facilities. The 'revolution' of free education which began 25 years ago has resulted in primary schools being introduced into most of Egypt's 4,000 villages. But the poor conditions of these schools and the high rate of 'absenteeism' of the pupils during agricultural peak seasons may explain the poor level of school-leavers, the majority of whom can safely be classified as

Table 5.11: Educational Status by Income Group

Household Groups	Total Population Size	Household Size	Educational Status										
			Less than Primary		Completed Primary		Completed Preparatory		Completed Secondary		Higher Education	
			No.	%	No.	%	No.	%	No.	%	No.	%
Poor	2 172	7.1	2 073	95.4	62	2.9	25	1.2	11	0.5	1	0.0
Marginal	957	5.3	919	96.0	24	2.5	12	1.3	2	0.2	—	—
Non-poor	2 008	4.8	1 760	87.6	97	4.8	63	3.1	74	3.7	14	0.7
Totals/averages	5 137	5.9	4 752	92.5	183	3.6	100	1.9	87	1.7	15	0.3

illiterate. Those who do well and want to continue their schooling have to go to the nearest city. They will have to take board under miserable conditions (with about five to a room), or commute every day using unbearably crowded means of transport or simply walking for a few kilometres. Moreover, the village is almost totally deprived of any cultural facilities. We know of no village in Egypt that has a cinema or a public library. Attempts to send 'culture-caravans' to the villages are sporadic and highly selective. The few copies of daily newspapers are usually read by a student to circles of illiterate peasants and 'transistor' radios (and sometimes a television set) provide a link with the outside world.

The picture outlined above of the conditions of housing and education are illustrative of the rest of basic needs. This reflects the pronounced 'urban bias' that characterised government policies for centuries. Social investment has always been concentrated in urban centres with little or no regard for the rural periphery beyond what was necessary for the mobilisation and extraction of the agricultural surplus. Attempts over the last quarter of a century to extend public services to the rural areas have undoubtedly led to some improvement but have fallen far short of redressing this imbalance.[29]

The Causes of Poverty

In the previous section we described some of the basic characteristics of poverty and noted the substantial inter-relationships between all variables considered. Here we shall discuss some of the factors that may explain the process of poverty generation such as the ownership of assets, employment, sources of income and demographic characteristics. It should be emphasised, however, that our distinction between characteristic and causative variables should not imply that the two categories are mutually exclusive. Low income, for instance, is as much a characteristic as a cause of poverty.

(a) Ownership of productive assets. It is an accepted fact that one of the main causes of rural poverty is the lack of access by the poor to productive assets, notably land.[30] The coincidence of growing poverty and landlessness in Egypt over the last quarter of a century must reflect the increasing deprivation of the rural population of access to land.[31] As we pointed out earlier, the highly skewed distribution of land ownership characteristic of rural Egypt since the establishment of private ownership of land has continued in the 1970s. The Gini coefficient for 1977 amounted to 0.556 compared to 0.432 in 1961 and 0.492 in 1952. For reasons explained earlier, these data should not lead to the

conclusion that land distribution has worsened, but that, at least, this distribution remained highly skewed as a result of the continued operation of disequalising tendencies since the land reform. In 1977, as in previous years, the majority of landowners were smallholders; 55.6 per cent of all ownerships were less than 1 feddan and accounted for 16.3 per cent of the land, and 94.2 per cent of ownerships were below 5 feddans and accounted for 68.2 per cent of the land. The top 5 per cent of ownerships accounted for 32 per cent of the land.

Given this general picture of inequality in the distribution of land ownership, it is not surprising that the results of our survey show a relatively limited access to land by the poor. Table 5.12 shows that the rural poor, who represented 35.3 per cent of rural households, owned 19.7 per cent of the total cultivated area, and the marginal group, 20.8 per cent of households, owned 12.9 per cent of the area. In other words, the poor and marginal groups, who make up 56 per cent of the rural households, owned only 32.5 per cent of the land. On the other hand, the non-poor, 44 per cent of households, owned 67.5 per cent of the land. The distribution of landholdings was not much less unequal than that of land ownership. Another feature of the structure of land distribution is the overwhelming prevalence of small holdings, especially among the poor. Our data show that while the average farm size for the whole sample was 2 feddans (which is about half the national average), the poor households operated holdings of about 1.5 feddans, and the holdings operated by the non-poor were about 2.5 feddans on average. Furthermore, the distribution of landholdings *among the poor* was highly unequal. About half the landholders in this category were very small farmers operating less than 1 feddan and held only 19 per cent of the land.

A corollary of the situation of unequal land distribution outlined above is the high incidence of landlessness among the poor. The difficulty of defining landlessness in an accurate way, given the high incidence of multiple economic activites among the rural households, was discussed earlier. But even on the basis of the strict definition of landlessness as the proportion of rural population engaged in agricultural activities and who do not own or operate land, we find that 25 per cent of the poor and marginal households engaged in agriculture were landless, while only 8.7 per cent of the non-poor would qualify for that description. Table 5.13 shows the diversity of activites pursued by landless households to generate income. It is very clear that, for the majority, the main source of income is wages earned from work on other farms in the village. It is interesting to note, however, that off-farm

Table 5.12 Distribution of Land Ownership and Landholding

Household Groups	Households in Each Group		Land Owned					Land Rented in				
			Owners		Area			Holders		Area		
	No.	%	No.	%	Kirats	%	Av. Area	No.	%	Kirats	%	Av. Area
Poor	306	35.3	94	30	2 736	20	29.1	124	41	3 710	38	30.0
Marginal	180	20.8	49	16	1 791	13	36.6	41	13	1 352	14	33.0
Non-poor	381	43.9	170	54	9 390	67	55.2	141	46	4 746	48	33.6
Totals/averages	867	100.0	313	100	13 917	100	44.5	306	100	9 808	100	32.1

Table 5.12 Distribution of Land Ownership and Landholding (contd)

Household Groups	Land Rented out					Total Landholding					
	Holders		Area			Holders		Area			
	No.	%	Kirats	%	Av. Area	No.	%	Kirats	%	Av. Area	
Poor	9	15	267	10	29.7	163	38	6 137	29	37.7	
Marginal	7	12	215	8	30.7	63	15	2 928	14	46.5	
Non-poor	43	73	2 286	82	53.2	201	47	11 839	57	59.0	
Totals/averages	59	100	2 768	100	47.0	427	100	20 904	100	49.0	

Table 5.13 Sources of Income for Landless Households

	Poor and Marginal Households		Non-poor Households	
	No.	Average Income (£E)	No.	Average Income (£E)
No. of agricultural households	339		195	
No. of landless households	86		17	
% of landless households	25.4		8.7	
Total income	86	215	17	315
Wages: other farms	85	160	15	195
Wages: off-farm in village	12	52	3	267
Wages: off-farm outside village	15	185	1	180
Earnings from agricultural products	43	8	14	11
Rent of land[a]	1	20	1	800
Income from non-agricultural assets	5	134	—	—
Remittances	17	25	1	100

Note: a. Cases of renting out land which was rented in the first place.

work, whether in or outside the village, was also an important source of income for some households, which reflects the importance of non-agricultural employment for the rural population. Another source of income of some importance, especially for poor households, was the income from non-agricultural assets. This reflects the importance of what we call the 'rural tertiary sector', where the rural poor, who face limited access to land and have no immediate prospect of employment in the urban sector, take refuge by engaging themselves in handicraft and trading activities. Finally, comment must be made on the one case where the family derives a substantial income (£E800) from renting in land to rent it out. Though this phenomenon of rural 'rentiers' has virtually disappeared under the pressure of growing demand for land, it is reminiscent of an erstwhile widespread practice when intermediaries rented large plots of land from absentee landlords only to rent it out in smaller parcels, making a good income from rent differentials.

The unequal distribution of land ownership was matched by even greater inequality in the distribution of other assets. Poor and marginal groups, who represent 56 per cent of rural households, had access to 36 per cent of the total productive assets, while the non-poor, 44 per cent of households, controlled 64 per cent of the assets (Table 5.14). The value of the Gini coefficient for asset distribution among income groups amounted to 0.723, which is higher than that for land ownership (0.556). The differentiation between the poor and non-poor is perhaps more apparent in the structure of their respective asset holding. While, for both, land is by far the most important asset (accounting for 60 per cent of total assets), we find that 'non-agricultural assets' are relatively more important in the case of non-poor households. This category of assets includes such things as the house, the establishment, non-agricultural land, etc. While the average value of a house for the poor is £E250, that of the non-poor was over £E600. Moreover, the average value of the 23 establishments owned by the poor amounted to £E150, while that of the 33 owned by the non-poor was £E944. These large differences in the value of establishments reflect the difference in the type of activities carried out by the poor and the non-poor. While the former are engaged in what we called the rural tertiary sector activities such as handicrafts and petty trade, the latter operate fairly large businesses such as livestock trading and transport companies. As we shall see later, the income generated from these types of assets differs substantially.

This disparity in the distribution of land and other productive assets must have serious implications for income distribution. We have seen

Table 5.14: Ownership of Productive Assets

Household Groups	No.	Total Assets			Farming Assets[a]			Land			Non-agricultural Assets		
		Total Value (£E)	% to Total	Mean Value (£E)	Total Value (£E)	% to Total	Mean Group Value (£E)	Total Value (£E)	% to Total	Mean Group Value (£E)	Total Value (£E)	% to Total	Mean Group Value (£E)
Poor	306	310 952	25	1 016	43 440	14	142	196 490	63	2 090	71 022	23	232
Marginal	180	137 548	11	764	27 966	20	155	76 313	55	1 557	33 269	24	185
Non-poor	381	809 456	64	2 125	90 185	11	237	480 708	59	2 828	238 563	30	628
Totals/averages	867	1 257 956	100	1 501	161 591	13	186	753 511	60	2 408	342 854	27	428

Note: a. Excluding land.

how assets were concentrated in a few households; the Gini coefficient for the size-distribution of all assets was as high as 0.725. We have also observed from the results of regression between household income and assets that variations in household incomes can largely be explained by the differences in asset ownership.[32] Table 5.15 sums up the situation: the strong positive correlation between the value of assets and both household and per capita incomes. The implications are very clear: assets are important sources of income generation and any improvements in income distribution would not be possible without some measure of asset redistribution.

Table 5.15:   Relationship between Assets and Income

Household Groups	Average Value of Assets (£E)	Average Income		Household Size
		Household (£E)	Per Capita (£E)	
Poor	1 016	327	46.0	7.1
Marginal	764	267	50.4	5.3
Non-poor	2 125	486	93.5	5.2
Total/average	1 501	384	65.0	5.9

(b) Demographic factors and employment characteristics. Demographic factors: It should be emphasised from the outset that we do not subscribe to the view that poverty is primarily *caused by* demographic factors in general and rapid population growth in particular.[33] It is our belief, however, that these factors which are largely the product of the poverty situation can partly 'explain' the process of poverty generation, a point which we shall try to illustrate using the few relevant data collected in the survey.

As pointed out earlier, the major demographic features of the population in our sample are strikingly similar to those of the total rural population. Thus we find that household members are divided into two equal halves between males and females, with the share of males slightly lower (49 per cent) in the case of poor and marginal households, and slightly higher (51 per cent) for the non-poor (Table 5.16). Similarly, the distribution of population by age conforms to the familiar pyramidal shape where 45 per cent of the population are below the age of 15; 51 per cent between 15 and 65; and a small proportion of 4 per cent over the age of 65.[34] What is more significant perhaps is the difference in age structure between various income groups. Table 5.16

Table 5.16: Age Structure

Age Groups	Total Population		Poor and Marginal Population		Non-poor Population	
	No.	%	No.	%	No.	%
Less than 1	240	4.7	146	4.7	94	4.7
1-3	384	7.5	238	7.6	146	7.3
4-6	494	9.6	320	10.2	174	8.7
7-9	368	7.2	250	8.0	118	5.9
10-12	469	9.1	322	10.3	147	7.3
13-15	344	6.7	230	7.4	114	5.7
16-19	396	7.7	229	7.3	167	8.3
20-39	1 322	25.7	730	23.3	592	29.5
40-49	393	7.7	249	8.0	144	7.2
50-59	355	6.9	209	6.6	146	7.3
60-64	153	3.0	80	2.6	73	3.5
65-69	72	1.4	37	1.2	35	1.7
More than 70	147	2.8	89	2.8	58	2.9
Total	5 137	100.0	3 129	100.0	2 008	100.0
Less than 15		45		48		40
16-64		51		48		56
More than 65		4		4		4
Males		49		51		50
Females		51		49		50

shows that poor and marginal families have to support a proportionately larger number of young population than the non-poor. The share of the age group of less than 15 years amounted to 48 per cent of the population of the former and 40 per cent of that of the latter. The corollary of this phenomenon is a lower proportion of the population of working age, 15-65, for poor and marginal households (48 per cent) than for the non-poor (56 per cent).

An important implication of this age structure is its effect on the dependency ratio. Table 5.17 shows that the dependency ratio (defined as the ratio of dependents — children below 15 years, adults above 65 years, students, disabled and the unemployed – to the total labour force (excluding wives) for the rural population as a whole amounted to 2.4.[35] Variations among income groups and occupational categories are significant. Thus, the dependency ratio for the poor households (2.8) was higher than for the population as a whole, reflecting the weight of a large proportion of dependents. These variations are important in view of the direct relationship between poverty and dependency at the household level resulting from the direct effect of dependency on real incomes.[36] Moreover, the ratio was higher among households headed by government employees, those working in services and craftsmen, while the ratio for agricultural households was about the same as the average. This can be explained by the fact that the former category of households, which happens to command relatively higher income as we shall see, has a higher proportion of students, while the children of agricultural households tend to find employment of some sort.

Table 5.17: Dependency Ratio by Occupation of Household Head[a]

Occupation of Household Head	Poor Households		All Households	
	Dependency Ratio	No. of Households	Dependency Ratio	No. of Households
Housewife	1.3	12	0.8	74
Farmer	2.7	137	2.5	318
Farm labourer	2.9	58	2.4	112
Craftsman	3.0	26	3.0	60
Construction	2.5	2	1.6	19
Services	3.5	15	2.6	61
Government	3.6	21	3.1	105
Others	2.3	17	2.6	48
Disabled	1.9	14	2.2	56
Regular army	—	—	4.3	3
Conscript	2.7	3	1.6	9
Student	2.5	1	1.3	2
Total	2.8	306	2.4	867

Note: a. Dependency ratio defined as the ratio of dependants (children below 15 years, adults above 65 years, students, disabled and the unemployed) to the total labour force, excluding housewives.

Finally, comment must be made on the observed variation in household size between the various income groups, as this has direct bearing on intra-household distribution of income and consumption. In Egypt, as in all other countries of the Third World, we have observed an direct relationship between household size and income, with the average size increasing from 1.6 for the lowest income group to 12.5 for the top income group. The crucial point to ascertain here is whether this direct relationship between household size and income implies an inverse correlation between household size and per capita incomes and, therefore, that a household in the lower income groups may not necessarily be classified as poor, even if small in size, as per capita income will be higher. For this to be true, the income elasticity of household size should be greater than unity. Using our survey data we came to the following results:

$$\log H = -1.4465 + 0.6566 \log Y$$
$$\quad\quad\quad (0.5371) \quad\ (0.0209)$$
$$R^2 = 0.4312$$
$$n = 867$$

where: H is household size

Y is household income.

It is clear that the income elasticity of household size, though positive, is less than unity (0.6566) and, therefore, total and per capita incomes cannot be inversely correlated. Table 5.18 shows that the poor are poor on account of both household and per capita incomes.

Employment characteristics: It is not our intention to deal with the questions of employment and the labour market in any detail at this stage. This will be the subject of Chapter 6. Here we shall present a profile of the basic employment characteristics of the poor, focusing mainly on the relationship between employment and the process of poverty generation.

Table 5.18:   Relationship between Household Size and Income

	Poor and Marginal Households	Non-poor Households	Total Households
Total population	3 129	2 008	5 137
No. of households	486	381	867
Household size	6.4	5.3	5.9
Household income (£E)	305	486	384
Income per capita (£E)	48	92	65

Table 5.19 sums up some of the main indices of the labour force. The picture that emerges is typical of many developing countries: a relatively low activity ratio of agricultural to total labour force. It is surprising that in the rural sector of a predominantly agricultural economy, agriculture provides only 55 per cent of the total employment opportunities. To explain this phenomenon we have to go beyond the 'sterile' activity rates to a wider analysis of the occupational structure of the rural households.

It is clear from Table 5.20 that while agricultural activities are the main providers of employment, 34 per cent of the labour force being self-employed farmers and 15 per cent agricultural wage earners, we

Table 5.19: Labour Force Indices

		Poor and Marginal Households	Non-poor Households	Total Households
1.	No. of households	486	381	867
2.	Population	3 129	2 008	5 137
3.	Population over 6 years	2 425	1 594	4 019
4.	Total labour force	1 888	1 236	3 124
5.	Labour force, excluding wives	974	621	1 595
6.	Civilian labour force	1 723	1 142	2 865
7.	Civilian labour force, excluding wives	809	527	1 336
8.	Agricultural labour force	577	306	883
9.	Crude activity rate $= 5 \div 2$ (%)	31	30	30[a]
10.	Refined activity rate $= 5 \div 3$ (%)	40	39	38[a]
11.	Agricultural to total labour force, excluding wives $= 8 \div 5$ (%)	59	49	55

Note: a. Similar figures for rural Egypt as a whole are 29 per cent and 37 per cent respectively; based on data from CAPMS: *Census of population and housing, 1976, detailed results*, Cairo, September 1978.

Table 5.20: Distribution of Labour Force by the Occupation of Household Head

	Poor and Marginal Households		Non-poor Households		Total Households	
	No.	%	No.	%	No.	%
Farmer	385	39.5	262	42.2	647	40.6
Farm labourer	192	19.7	44	7.1	236	14.8
Craftsman	72	7.4	48	7.7	120	7.5
Construction worker	15	1.5	14	2.3	29	1.8
Service worker	44	4.5	42	6.7	86	5.4
Government employee	51	5.2	97	15.6	148	9.3
Others	50	5.1	20	3.2	70	4.4
Regular army	4	0.3	13	2.1	17	1.1
National service	55	5.6	41	6.6	96	6.0
Looking for work	20	2.1	10	1.6	30	1.9
Total labour force, excluding wives[a]	974	100.0	621	100.0	1 595	100.0

Note: a. Total shares of various occupations may not add up to 100 per cent of the labour force due to differences in classifications.

find that two other sets of occupations are not less important. First, there is what we may loosely call the secondary and tertiary sectors of the rural areas which include such activities as small and cottage industries and handicrafts, trade and services, which provide some 20 per cent of total employment. Secondly, there is the government sector where about 10 per cent of the labour force finds employment. This phenomenon of increasing rural employment is neither new nor unique to Egypt. With the stagnation of agriculture, mainly as a result of reaching the arable land frontier, and the rapid increase in population, a process of 'tertiarisation' began to take place, where the new entrants to the labour force who are unable to find employment in agriculture or the opportunity to migrate to urban centres joined the ranks of the tertiary sector in handicrafts and petty trade, catering for the needs of the rural population. Meanwhile, the vast expansion of the economic functions of the State, especially as a result of agrarian reform and the creation of a large public sector in the 1960s, created new employment opportunities both in and outside the villages. Given the phenomenal urban congestion, many of those who work outside the village prefer to take residence in their village and commute daily to work. The employment structure, therefore, reflects not only the crisis in agriculture but also the impact of a certain pattern of development common to Third World countries.

These general employment characteristics should not blur the important differences among income groups. Table 5.19 shows that agricultural employment was more important for the poor than for the non-poor. While it represented 59 per cent for the former, it amounted to 49 per cent for the latter, the difference being due to the higher proportion of poor who are agricultural wage earners (Table 5.20). On the other hand government employment is much less (5.2 per cent) for the poor than for the non-poor (15.6 per cent). Moreover, both the rate of open unemployment (2.1 per cent) and underemployment (35 per cent) for the poor are higher than for the non-poor (1.6 per cent and 28 per cent respectively). Underemployment was gauged by asking the question 'Do you think you could have worked more over the last year?' The rate of underemployment was thus calculated as the percentage of those answering in the affirmative to total labour force. It is obvious that estimates based on answers of this attitudinal question should not be considered more than indicative and provide no substitute for a time-use study.

Another important aspect of the differentiation between various income groups is the differences in incomes generated from employment.

Table 5.21:   Average Income by Occupation of Household Head

Occupation of Household Head	Poor and Marginal Households			Non-poor Households			Total Households		
	No.	%	Average Household Income (£E)	No.	%	Average Household Income (£E)	No.	%	Average Household Income (£E)
Housewife	31	6.4	172	43	11.3	340	74	8.5	269
Farmer	184	37.9	363	134	35.2	594	318	36.7	460
Farm labourer	93	19.1	218	19	5.0	339	112	13.0	239
Craftsman	34	7.0	320	26	6.8	495	60	6.9	396
Construction worker	8	1.6	405	11	2.9	345	19	2.2	370
Service worker	29	6.0	249	32	8.4	562	61	7.0	413
Government employee	36	7.4	400	69	18.1	469	105	12.2	446
Others	32	6.6	334	16	4.2	360	48	5.5	343
Disabled	35	7.2	220	21	5.5	346	56	6.5	266
Regular army	—	—	—	3	0.7	579	3	0.3	579
National service	3	0.6	402	6	1.6	407	9	1.0	405
Student	1	0.2	342	1	0.3	160	2	0.2	250
Totals/averages	486	100.0	305	381	100.0	486	867	100.0	384

Two major observations emerge from the evidence provided in Table 5.21 on the relationship between employment and income. The first is that the working members of poor households tend to be concentrated in relatively low-income occupations. We note that 19 per cent are agricultural wage earners, 6 per cent service workers, 7 per cent in handicrafts and another 7 per cent are disabled. Incomes from these jobs are either below or around the poverty-line income. Secondly, the members of poor households engaged in the same occupation as the non-poor get lower incomes, examples being farmers, craftsmen and government employees. The explanation is simple: the non-poor farmers own larger plots of land, craftsmen have larger workshops and government employees have a higher status in the civil service. The existence of these differentials points to the futility of depending on employment data alone for the analysis of poverty. Employment should be related to the income it generates for us to be able to draw meaningful conclusions. This point will be further elaborated in the next section.

(c) Sources of income. Numerous studies on rural poverty in developing countries single out the ownership of productive assets, especially land, as the main source of income, and tend to explain poverty in terms of the unequal distribution of such assets and the lack of access by the poor to them and the incomes they generate.[37] There is no doubt, as demonstrated in section (a) above, that differences in asset ownership explain a significant proportion of the variation in incomes. But asset ownership alone cannot explain all these variations. In fact, the results of the present survey show that, for the rural population as a whole, income generated from assets (including labour input for owner-operated land) amounted to less than half (48.3 per cent) of the total earnings. Income from land alone amounted to 36 per cent and the remaining part mainly from earnings from non-agricultural productive assets (Table 5.22). The striking feature of the distribution of income by source is the remarkably high proportion of earnings (46 per cent) generated from wage-employment in and outside the village. This is not surprising in view of what we observed earlier about half the labour force being engaged in non-agricultural activities.

The differences in income sources between the poor and non-poor households are significant. While the non-poor derive 53 per cent of their earnings from the ownership of assets and 47 per cent from wage-employment and remittances, the order is almost reversed in the case of the poor and marginal households; 43 per cent from assets, 53 per cent from wages and 4 per cent from remittances. A closer look at the

Table 5.22: Sources of Income

Sources of Income	Poor and Marginal Households				Non-poor Households				Total Households			
	No. of Households	Value (£E)	%	Average per Household (£E)	No. of Households	Value (£E)	%	Average per Household (£E)	No. of Households	Value (£E)	%	Average per Household (£E)
Earnings from family farm	357	51 371	34.7	144	287	67 689	36.7	236	644	119 060	35.8	185
Wages: other farms	222	28 967	19.6	130	83	11 880	6.4	143	305	40 846	12.3	134
Wages: off-farm in village	92	15 346	10.4	167	72	15 537	8.4	216	164	30 883	9.3	188
Wages: off-farm outside village	119	33 590	22.7	282	142	47 674	25.8	336	261	81 264	24.4	311
Rent of land	15	797	0.5	53	39	3 738	2.0	96	54	4 535	1.4	84
Rent of equipment	5	171	0.1	34	16	3 163	1.7	198	21	3 334	1.0	159
Non-agricultural assets	51	11 590	7.8	227	47	21 715	11.8	462	98	33 305	10.0	340
Rental of house owned	—	—	—	—	2	342	0.2	162	2	324	0.1	162
Remittances	120	5 723	3.9	48	111	11 679	6.3	105	201	17 402	5.2	87
Totals/averages	486	148 149	100.0	305	380	184 641	100.0	486	866	332 790	100.0	384

sources of incomes of the poor shows that the most important source of income after earnings from the family farm was wages for employment outside the village followed by employment on other farms in the village. Wages from off-farm activities in the village and non-agricultural assets must reflect the poor's attempt to earn a living by providing services or being engaged in handicrafts and petty trade. Finally, we note that remittances have become an important source of income (5 per cent). Many families in rural Egypt now have somebody working either in towns or in rich oil-producing Arab countries who sends back part of his salary to support the family.

The picture that emerges from the above analysis has extremely important implications both for our understanding of poverty and for policy recommendations. It is clear that in a country like Egypt, with a rapidly growing population and a fixed supply of arable land, employment becomes an important source of income generation, perhaps as important as produtive assets. Moreover, it appears that a process of 'tertiarisation' has been taking place in rural Egypt where the poor who face limited access to land and have little prospect of being absorbed in the urban economy try to earn their living by engaging in such low productivity activities as handicrafts and petty trade. In view of all this, any anti-poverty policy should have as its aim, besides achieving a more equitable distribution of assets, the creation of productive employment opportunities in rural non-agricultural activities and the raising of earnings from wage-employment.

Recent developments in rural Egypt, while introducing fundamental changes, do not invalidate the above-mentioned conclusion. The main sources of change since the mid-1970s have been: (a) the mass emigration to oil-rich Arab countries and the consequent spurt in remittances; and (b) the increase in the demand for labour, both due to emigration and the construction boom in urban areas, which led to the emergence of a labour shortage in what used to be a labour surplus economy. These two changes had far-reaching effects on income distribution and poverty in rural Egypt (see Chapter 7). The 1980s have witnessed a situation where the groups that were traditionally described as poor – the wage labourers – have enjoyed an improvement in their position as a result of the increase in rural wages. Moreover, the labour-endowed households with adult members working in oil-rich Arab countries climbed up the income distribution ladder thanks to the remittances sent to them. The other side of the picture was represented by the consequences on the very small landholders (the near-landless) who were unable to join the ranks of emigrants and were locked in their tiny holdings. This group, together with the members of what we call the tertiary sector, represented the new poor in rural Egypt.

The difference then between the situation in the early 1970s and the 1980s is a qualitative one in the sense that groups have changed places in the income distribution matrix, but the fundamental characteristics of the agrarian system remain more or less the same. Moreover, our conclusion on the importance of employment creation as an anti-poverty policy is strengthened by the fact that remittances and increased wages are based on uncertain developments: the possibility to emigrate and the construction boom. There is always a danger that these sources might spend their force in case migrants return and/or the construction boom comes to an end. Thus any policy aiming at hedging the poor against violent fluctuations should have non-agricultural rural employment creation as one of its major objectives.

Appendix: Basic Needs in an Egyptian Village: the Case of Kamalia

Introduction

Egyptian village society remained neglected as a field of study until the pioneering work of Ayrout on the 'Egyptian Peasant' which appeared in the late 1930s.[38] This study was a sympathetic, yet paternalistic, traveller's account of the manners and customs of the fellahin. Since then at least five serious village studies have appeared: Abbas Ammar, in reaction to the early signals of 'population explosion', focused on the demographic features of the villages in his province, Sharqiya;[39] Hamed Ammar in his study of his native village, Silwa, provided, for the first time, some empirical foundations for the well-known misery of the fellah in upper Egypt;[40] Jacque Berque provided the most vivid picture of social norms in his study of Sirs El-Layyan;[41] H. Fakhouri observed both the strain and the response of a traditional village, Kafr El-Elow, to rapid industrialisation;[42] and Iliya Harik attempted to monitor the effect of politicisation on the village community.[43] Despite the marked divergence between these studies both in method and approach, we find that they have two common characteristics. *First*, the method of investigation is based either on casual observation or questionnaires dealing with attitudinal questions. *Secondly*, the emphasis is invariably on cultural norms and social habits, and seldom on the economic basis of life in the village. In this Appendix we try to go beyond this approach and investigate the economic infrastructure of village society, without losing sight of the importance of the villagers' perceptions of the consequent superstructures: hierarchy, social relations, government, etc.

In this Appendix we shall present a very brief description of economic conditions in one of the 18 villages covered by our survey. The basic information was obtained from a day-long discussion with villagers and their leaders and this is supplemented by data for the same village from the survey proper. Since the basic information was obtained from discussion with a group whose representativeness was unknown to us and the accuracy of information was not cross-checked, we make no claim of scientific accuracy for our results. Rather, the intention is to present a broad impression of what poverty means in the context of an Egyptian village, as perceived by some villagers.

The discussions were held in the house of the Umda (village headman) and most of the village council were present. Although the leaders took a prominent part in these discussions, there were also 20 to 30 other villagers present, who appeared poor and who were described as such by the leaders. Many among this group also took an active part in the discussion.

The Village

Kamalia is a relatively small Egyptian village, with a population of about 2,500, living in 386 households, and is situated 9 kilometres from the town of Mahalla El-Kubra in the Nile delta. Despite its proximity to an urban centre (the largest textile-manufacturing complex in the country) it is primarily an agricultural village, growing cotton and a variety of food crops. It consists of 700 feddans of cultivable land and thus has a land/man ratio of 0.28 feddan per resident which is close to the national average figure of 0.29 feddan per person in 1976.

From the survey data for Kamalia, which covered 10 per cent of the total number of households in the village, we are able to construct the following picture of economic conditions in the village. The average annual income per household was £E399, slightly higher than the average of £E384 for the whole sample. Incomes were, however, highly unequally distributed: the Gini coefficient of size-distribution of household incomes was 0.447. As was the case for the survey as a whole, household size was positively related to household income and the degree of inequality was lower when allowance was made for this factor (see Table A5.1).

A striking feature of the per capita income distribution figures was that three basic income groups are identifiable. A majority of households (the bottom 70 per cent) had a per capita household income of less than £E48, which was clearly below the per capita poverty line of £E67. Above this was a group (27 per cent) of households which had a per capita income that was roughly double that of the poverty group. Finally, there were the village rich, represented by the top 3 per cent, who had a per capita income that was considerably higher than the rest.

Table A5.1:   Kamalia: Distribution of Land

Kirats	Holdings		Ownership		
	No.	Average Size	No.	Average Size	Total
Less than 24.0	9	19.7	5	15.4	77.0
24.0-47.9	8	44.0	2	36.0	72.0
48.0-71.9	2	62.0	1	60.0	60.0
72.0-95.9	3	88.0	1	96.0	96.0
96.0-119.9	—	—	1	120.0	120.0
120.0-143.9	2	144.0	—	—	—
144.0-191.9	—	—	—	—	—
192.0-239.9	1	240.0	—	—	—
240.0-360.0	1	264.0	1	360.0	360.0
Total averages		65.73		71.7	789.0
Total nos. and areas	26	1 709	11	789	

Table A5.2:   Kamalia: Distribution of Income

Income Class (£E)	No. of Households	Mean Income (£E)	Average Household Size	Mean Income per Capita (£E)
More than 50.0	2	37.8	1.00	37.8
75.0-99.9	1	94.8	2.00	47.4
100.0-149.9	4	120.5	4.75	25.4
150.0-199.9	7	185.2	5.57	33.2
200.0-249.9	2	227.1	6.50	34.9
250.0-299.9	4	277.3	7.25	38.2
300.0-349.9	4	332.7	8.25	40.3
500.0-599.9	1	562.5	7.00	80.4
600.0-799.9	4	645.7	7.75	83.3
800.0-999.9.	1	811.4	9.00	90.2
1 000.0-1 399.9	3	1 014.8	10.70	94.8
1 400.0-2 000.0	1	1 734.5	7.00	247.8
Totals/averages	34	399	6.56	60.8

The main characteristics of poverty in Kamalia are not much different from those observed for the sample as a whole (Table A5.2). Thus we find that of the 43 households surveyed, 71 per cent, representing 65 per cent of the population, live in poverty (i.e. their per capita income falls below the poverty line income of £E67). The unequal distribution of income between poor and non-poor households is reflected in these groups' disproportionate shares in total income: 56 per cent of total income went to the 29 per cent non-poor households (with a mean income of £E758), while only 44 per cent went to the 71 per cent poor households (with a mean income of £E250). Other attributes of poverty conform to the general picture. The consumption pattern of the poor is dominated by expenditure on food (66 per cent of total expenditure) and their diet is cereal-based (26 per cent of total expenditure). The incidence of illiteracy is higher among the poor (92 per cent have 'less than primary education') than the non-poor (86 per cent). Differentiation is perhaps most evident in housing conditions.

Table A5.3:   Kamalia: Main Characteristics of Poverty

	Poor Households	Non-poor Households	Total
No. of households	24	10	34
No. of household members	146	77	223
Household size	6.1	7.7	6.6
Income per household (£E)	250	758	70
Income per capita (£E)	49	121	399
% of those with less than primary education	92	86	91
Average household expenditure (£E)	238	570	336
% expenditure on food	66	48	61
% expenditure on cereals	26	16	23
% of houses with potable water	—	10	3
% of houses with electricity	21	50	29
% of houses with toilets	38	80	50
Average no. of rooms per house	2.9	4.4	3.3
Density – persons per room	2.4	1.5	2.1

Thus we find that none of the poor households have access to clean drinking water, 38 per cent of the houses have toilets and only 21 per cent have electricity. Finally, the survey results for Kamalia confirm our general conclusion that poverty is closely associated with lack of access to productive assets, especially land, as well as regular

Table A5.4:   Kamalia Sources of Income by Income Class

Income Class (£E)	No. of House-holds	Wage / Other Farms		Wage Off-farm in Village		Wage Off-farm Outside		Family Farm	
		X	Y	X	Y	X	Y	X	Y
Less than 50.0	2	—	—	—	—	—	—	1	21
50.0-74.9	—	—	—	—	—	—	—	—	—
75.0-99.9	1	1	9.0	—	—	—	—	1	14
100.0-149.9	4	3	82.7	—	—	1	45	2	85
150.0-199.9	7	6	101.3	—	—	1	180	6	70
200.0-249.9	2	2	60.0	—	—	1	108	2	98
250.0-299.9	4	2	153.0	—	—	1	108	4	174
300.0-349.9	4	3	53.3	—	—	1	345	3	268
350.0-399.9	—	—	—	—	—	—	—	—	—
400.0-499.9	—	—	—	—	—	—	—	—	—
500.0-599.9	4	1	56.0	—	—	1	270	1	237
600.0-799.9	1	1	24.0	1	108	4	300	4	279
800.0-999.9	1	—	—	—	—	1	520	1	220
1 000.0-1 399.9	3	—	—	—	—	1	270	3	758
1 400.0-2 000.0	1	—	—	—	—	1	470	1	464
Total village	34	19	80.6	1	108	13	270	29	229

Note: X = No. of households.   Y = Mean income from each source.

Table A5.4: Kamalia Sources of Income by Income Class (contd)

Income Class (£E)	Rent of Land		Rent for Equipment and Livestock		Non-agriculture		Remittances	
	X	Y	X	Y	X	Y	X	Y
Less than 50.0	—	—	—	—	—	—	2	27.5
50.0-74.9	—	—	—	—	—	—	—	—
75.0-99.9	—	—	—	—	—	—	1	72.0
100.0-149.9	—	—	—	—	—	—	1	20.0
150.0-199.9	—	—	—	—	—	—	—	—
200.0-249.9	—	—	—	—	—	—	1	30.0
250.0-299.9	—	—	—	—	—	—	—	—
300.0-349.9	—	—	—	—	—	—	1	24.0
350.0-399.9	—	—	—	—	—	—	—	—
400.0-499.9	—	—	—	—	—	—	—	—
500.0-599.9	1	110	—	—	—	—	—	—
600.0-799.9	—	—	—	—	1	50	—	—
800.0-999.9	1	150	—	—	—	—	1	48.0
1 000.0-1399.9	1	150	2	140	—	—	1	48.0
1 400.0-2 000.0	—	—	1	800	—	—	—	—
Total village	2	130	3	360	1	50	8	37.1

employment in non-agricultural activites. The main source of income for the village poor appears to be wages from work on other farms and, to a much lesser extent, remittances.

The sources of income for Kamalia are varied but agricultural income constitutes a much higher proportion (almost 70 per cent) of total income than for the sample as a whole. Of total incomes, 49 per cent comes from family farms, 11 per cent from wage-earnings on other farms, while another 10 per cent comes from the rent of land, agricultural equipment and livestock. Most of the remainder of total income comes from off-farm earnings outside the village. This low level of off-farm wage-earnings is surprising considering the proximity of the village to Mahalla, the largest industrial centre in the country.

There is a broad association between sources of income and its overall level. Almost all cases of wage-earnings from agricultural labour occur in the poverty group and 70 per cent of poor households have earnings from this source. On the other hand, all rental income accrues to the non-poor and the relative incidence of off-farm earnings is much higher for the non-poor (80 per cent of households versus 20 per cent for the poor).

Only one-third of the households in Kamalia own any land and even within this group land ownership is highly concentrated; one out of the eleven households which are shown as owning land accounts for almost 50 per cent of total land owned. Tenancy increases substantially the number of households with access to land but about one-quarter of the households still remain as landless, i.e. without a landholding of any sort. Almost all of these landless households are in the poverty group.

Thus in Kamalia it is access to land and agricultural assets as well as to high-income off-farm employment outside the village which determines the income differences between rich and poor.

Perceptions of Poverty and Basic Needs

The above picture of income distribution and poverty was built up from our survey results and our independently based estimates of the poverty line for the whole sample but, quite remarkably, it also coincides very closely with the perceptions of the villagers on these issues. When asked what they considered constituted a poverty level, they answered that £E5 per person per month was the minimum income that was required to keep a family above the poverty level. Our independent estimate of the poverty line for the sample as a whole was £E67 per capita. The estimate of the number of poor people in the village ('much more than half') was also consistent with our estimate based on the survey data. Similarly, this estimate that one-quarter of all households in the village were landless coincides almost exactly with ours.

The responses to questions about what they considered to be basic requirements were a poignant reminder of the pitifully low levels of living in the village. The four main complaints related to a shortage of food, overcrowded housing, a lack of sufficient clothing and the wide prevalence of bilharzia and ophthalmic diseases. These deprivations were sometimes eloquently expressed; the monotony of the average diet was described by saying that 'meat is one of the prohibitions' while the shortage of clothing was summed up by the statement that 'washing and waiting' was a normal occurrence. While these deprivations were keenly felt, the aspirations, as reflected in their answers on what they considered to be minimum requirements, were very modest. They felt that they needed a more varied diet than that of only cereals and cheese. In addition, they felt that poor families should each get 2 kilograms of cereals over and above what they have at present – probably an indication of general awareness of calorific deficiency among the poor. In terms of clothing, they felt that each person should have two *galabias*, two pairs of underwear and a pair of slippers, while, for housing, they felt that each family should have at least two rooms – one for the couple and the other for the children. These are indeed modest targets, yet they constitute the stuff of aspirations for the very poor.

These deprivations in private consumption were matched by deficiencies in terms of socially provided services such as health, education and sanitation. Information on health and other facilities was given in full consciousness of the inadequacy of the present situation. There was no clinic or medical centre in the village and the nearest source of medical attention was at the government hospital in Mahalla, half an hour away by bus. Although treatment was free at the hospital, long periods of waiting were a frequent occurrence. The only alternative to the hospital was to go to private doctors in town, who charged between £E0.50 to £E1 per consultation. These are very high fees in relation to the per capita household incomes in the village: between 10 and 20 per cent of the average monthly per capita household income.

There were no schools in the village. The nearest primary school was three-quarters of a kilometre away and the nearest preparatory school was 3 kilometres away. The costs of education incurred by the household were extremely high in relation to per capita incomes; it was estimated that school fees and other expenses amounted to £E1 per month for a child at primary school. Not surprisingly, there is a very high drop-out rate after one or at most two years at primary school.

The only source of clean water was three standpipes in a neighbouring village three-quarters of a kilometre away. When these standpipes function normally, water supply is not seen as a problem. However, breakdowns which last two to three days are frequent and cause great inconvenience.

Electricity has been introduced into the village, but only a minority of houses have individual connections; the cost of installation (£E15-19) is prohibitive to the poor. Kerosene is therefore the most common source of light. For fuel, cotton and maize stalks are used.

Overcrowded housing, as we have mentioned, was a common complaint, yet all but 15 houses in the village were very simple structures made of mud-bricks, which, it seemed to us, were easily amenable to own-construction at minimal cost. On further discussion, however, we found that the cash payment that was required for even these structures was high. Payments necessary to cover the fees of the brick-maker and the carpenter, and the cost of wood for ceilings, doors and windows amounted to £E130 for a simple two-room structure. In Kamalia, therefore, housing was no longer a self-reliant activity, requiring the mere investment of one's labour.

Local Government

Kamalia is, in theory, governed by a village council, but in practice its affairs are decided by the bureaucracy. Government employees dominate the village council, which in any case has a budget of only £E20 to £E30 to dispose of. There are no village projects or any initiatives to improve economic conditions in the village.

Apart from the village council, the village has an 'Umda', or headman, who represents the traditional power structure of the village. The Umda of Kamalia was an intelligent and impressive man, but he came from probably the wealthiest family in the village and the 'Umdaship' had been hereditary within his family for several generations. In fact, in all the villages covered by the survey, the Umda came from one of the wealthiest families and the function had been hereditary within the family for at least two generations.

The Umda and a young man representing the Arab Socialist Union[44] expressed strong views about the need for development projects in the village, but there was also a fatalistic cynicism about anything happening. They saw their role as transmitters of requests to the government and not as mobilisers of effort within the village itself. A prime grievance of long standing was the problem of inadquate soil drainage and the consequent waterlogging and soil salinity. Kamalia stood at the end of a little branch canal and, as a consequence, was unable to discharge excess irrigation water. Yet the main drain itself was only 1 kilometre away and the village had constantly petitioned for the construction of another branch canal. These requests have invariably been turned down.

It would appear that here was a classic case where, relying only on its own resources, a village could achieve a highly beneficial piece of infrastructural construction. To view the matter thus, however, would be to ignore the web of bureaucratic restraints that exists. To undertake such a task, permission would be required and this has been consistently withheld. More generally, the pattern of agricultural production in the village is finely regulated. In October of each year the agricultural engineer arrives and, without consultation, divides the village land into basins and decrees the crop rotation. The announcement is made to villagers gathered at the village mosque. The seeds to be used for most of the crops grown in the village are also chosen by the Ministry and there is no room for individual experimentation or innovation. As for irrigation, there is an irrigation inspector for each 'markaz' (district) who decides on the rationing of water.

Perceptions of Economic Change

There was a general feeling that economic conditions in the village had worsened over the years. Population growth was identified as a major problem and was held to be responsible for declining land/man ratios and the overcrowded housing conditions. Furthermore, there were complaints that yields had been falling, due to increased crop damage from plant disease, locusts and increased soil salinity. It was also maintained that real wages had remained stagnant.

Some economic events were remembered but none were described as having brought about any significant improvement in the standard of living. The land reform was recalled, but it did not have a major impact in Kamalia; only 56 out of the 700 feddans were redistributed. The introduction of electricity, the bus service to Mahalla and the water supply were remembered, but only the latter was perceived as having had a significant beneficial impact in that it reduced the incidence of some diseases among the population. In the area of agricultural production, the one change which was mentioned, without any particular enthusiasm, was the introduction of a mechanised thresher owned by the co-operative to replace the traditional *norag*.

Conclusion

The overall impression we were left with was one of widespread poverty which was keenly felt and of a very modest level of aspiration among the poor. The latter is probably the result of the general stagnation that has endured in the village and a general cynicism about any significant change being brought about by the government. There was a general resignation to the facts of poverty in the fact of an entrenched traditional economic and political structure in the village and an indifferent bureaucracy.

Ensuring the satisfaction of basic needs in Kamalia would require far-reaching changes within the village, carried out in the context of similar changes in Egyptian rural society as a whole.

Notes

1. A measure of relative poverty could be defined in terms of the share of the lowest x per cent of population in total income. To use the often quoted figure, the share of the bottom 40 per cent of rural population in rural Egypt will amount to 16 per cent and the top 20 per cent to about 45 per cent of income. We find this measure of limited use in understanding poverty.

2. A. K. Sen: *Three notes on the concept of poverty*, World Employment Programme research working paper (WEP 2-23/WEP 65) (Geneva, ILO, 1978), p. 14.

3. WHO: *Energy and protein requirements*, Report of a Joint FAO/WHO *Ad Hoc* Committee, No. 522 (Geneva, 1973).

4. Appendix to Chapter 5.

5. FAO: *Fourth world food survey* (Rome, 1977), p. 78.

6. S. Radwan: *Agrarian reform and rural development: Egypt 1952-1975* (Geneva, ILO, 1977), p. 46.

7. The FAO estimates that in 1972-4, about 8 per cent of the population of Egypt were undernourished. Cf. FAO, *Fourth world food survey*, p. 127.

8. The value of the poverty-line income estimated here appears reasonable when compared with estimates for previous years. The figure for 1974/5 amounted to £E53.50. Given the rate of inflation of some 20 per cent for food according to official statistics, the figure of £E67 for 1977 appears reasonable.

9. The figure actually refers to consumption expenditure rather than income.

10. B. Seebohm Rowntree: *Poverty: A study of town life* (London, Macmillan, 1908), pp. 86-7.

11. Ibid., p. 87.

12. Similarly, one can talk of the calorie gap denoting the short fall of calorie intake from requirements. For details, see S. Reutlinger and M. Selowsky: *Malnutrition and poverty: Magnitude and policy options*, World Bank Staff Occasional Papers, No. 23 (Washington, DC, 1976).

13. For details, see A. K. Sen: 'Poverty: An ordinal approach to measurement', in *Econometrica*, March 1976; and S. Ananad: 'Aspects of poverty in Malaysia', in *Review of Income and Wealth*, March 1977.

14. Sen, 'Poverty', p. 219.

15. Sen, *Three notes*, p. 25.

16. A. K. Sen: 'Poverty, inequality and unemployment: Some conceptual issues in measurement', in *Economic and Political Weekly* (New Delhi), August 1973, p. 1463.

17. A similar categorisation was used by G. B. Rodgers: 'A conceptualization of poverty in rural India', in *World Development* (Oxford), vol. 4, no. 4, 1976.

18. The 'reference man' and 'reference woman' are hypothetical persons used to calculate energy requirements. For instance, a reference man according to the FAO/WHO definition is one between 20 and 39 years, weighs 65 kg and is engaged in moderate activity. See WHO, *Energy and protein requirements*, p. 12.

19. FAO, *Fourth world food survey*, Appendix C.

20. See, *inter alia*, Rodgers, 'Conceptualization of poverty', p. 263, and United Nations: *Poverty, unemployment and development policy: A case study of selected issues with reference to Kerala* (New York, 1975).

21. M. Abdel-Fadil: *Development, income distribution and social change in rural Egypt (1952-1970)*, Occasional Paper No. 45 (University of Cambridge, Department of Applied Economics, 1975), p. 76.

22. CAPMS: *1976 Population Census: Preliminary results* (Cairo, 1977), pp. 62-3.

23. Ibid., pp. 58 and 61.

24. Ibid, p. 58.

25. The comparable figure from the 1976 Population Census was 1-8 persons per room. These density ratios underestimate the real degree of crowdedness, since the definition of room includes halls, kitchens, cattle-sheds, etc.

26. For a fascinating description, see H. H. Ayoub: *The Egyptian peasant* (Boston, Beacon Press, 1968), and J. Berque: *Histoire sociale d'un village égyptian au XXème siècle* (Paris, Mouton, 1957).

27. Questions related to education in the survey were limited to this indicator. Other questions of functional literacy and physical access were not asked.

28. CAPMS, *Preliminary results, 1976*, p. 54.

29. Ministry of Planning: 'Indicators of regional development, 1964/5-1966/7, unpublished memorandum, Cairo, 1968, pp. 148-57.

30. ILO: *Poverty and landlessness in rural Asia* (Geneva, ILO, 1977).

31. For past developments, see Radwan, *Agrarian reform and rural development*.

32. The regression between income and ownership of assets gives the following result:

$$\log Y = 1.3343 + 0.5354 \log K$$
$$(0.7156)$$
$$R^2 = 0.286$$
$$n = 867$$

where: Y = household income
K = value of total assets (less financial assets).

33. For an excellent refutation of the demographic determinists' views, see the case study of an Indian village by M. Mamdani: *The myth of population control* (New York, Monthly Review Press, 1972).

34. These are very similar to the 1976 Population Census figures for rural Egypt as a whole.

35. This is the same figure as that for rural Egypt. See A. Nassef and F. Abdul-Kader: 'Analysis of labour force in Egpyt in 1966', in Cairo Demographic Centre: *Demographic aspects of manpower in Arab countries* (Cairo, 1972), Table 1, p. 136.

36. Rodgers, 'Conceptualization of poverty', p. 273, observed that among individuals in the Kosi area of India with calorie intakes of less than 50 per cent of recommended intakes, more than half had dependency ratios substantially in excess of the average.

37. See, *inter alia*, ILO, *Poverty and landlessness in rural Asia*, and K. B. Griffin: *The political economy of agrarian change* (London, Macmillan, 1973).

38. H. B. Ayrout: *The Egyptian peasant* (Boston, Beacon Press, 1968).

39. A. Ammar: *A demographic study of an Egyptian province (Sharqiya)* (London, London School of Economics and Political Science, 1942).

40. H. Ammar: 'Growing-up in an Egyptian village: Silwa, province of Aswan', London, mimeo., 1954.

41. Berque, *Histoire sociale d'un village égyptien*.

42. H. Fakhouri: *Kafr El-Elow: An Egyptian village in transition* (New York, Holt, Rinehart and Winston, 1972).

43. Iliya Harik: *The political mobilisation of peasants: A study of an Egyptian community* (Bloomington, Indiana, Indiana University Press, 1974).

44. Egypt's only party before the present multi-party system came into existence.

6 Employment and the Labour Market

Introduction

In this chapter, the survey results will be drawn upon to depict a picture of the broad features of the employment situation and the functioning of the labour market in rural Egypt. It should be emphasised from the outset that no attempt is made here to provide anything like a detailed analysis of labour force utilisation. This has been the subject of numerous other studies.[1] Our aim is rather limited and somewhat different: to analyse the dual relationship between the employment characteristics of the household and such factors as the household's ownership of assets, income, education, etc. Moreover, since employment is a major source of income for the poor households, we shall focus on the interaction between employment and income generation. Thus, the chapter will begin with a description of the pattern of rural employment; then an attempt will be made to explore the main features of the labour market in a poor agrarian economy by identifying the principal determinants of labour supply; and, finally, the major factors that influence rural wages will be analysed.

Patterns of Rural Employment

The general picture that emerges from Table 6.1, which sums up some of the conventional labour force indices for rural Egypt, is typical of many developing countries. First, we notice a relatively low activity ratio of 30 per cent, which reflects the impact of both the demographic structure and the employment situation. In rural Egypt, almost half the population (45 per cent) are below the age of 15. Moreover, despite the fact that employment figures are usually inflated since the majority of adults are reported as engaged in employment of some sort or the other, the dependency ratio remains as high as 2.4.[2] Secondly, the female participation ratio appears to be low. An indication of that is provided by the high proportion of 'housewives' (49 per cent) in the total labour force. To exclude these from the rural labour force is to reduce the labour force by half. Thirdly, the proportion of the labour force engaged in military service is somewhat high (about 16 per cent of the total labour force). This reflects the demand by the army on the working population resulting from the Middle East conflict prior to the recent developments.

Table 6.1:   Some Labour Force Indices

		Total Households
1.	No. of households	867
2.	Population	5 317
3.	Population above 6 years	4 019
4.	Total labour force	3 124
5.	Labour force, excluding wives	1 595
6.	Civilian labour force	2 865
7.	Civilian labour force, excluding wives	1 336
8.	Agricultural labour force	883
9.	Crude activity rate = 5 ÷ 2 (%)	30[a]
10.	Refined activity rate =5 ÷ 3 (%)	38[a]
11.	Agricultural to total labour force excluding wives = 8 ÷ 5 (%)	55

Note: a. Similar figures for rural Egypt as a whole are 29 per cent and 37 per cent respectively.

The striking feature of the occupational structure which emerges from Table 6.1 is what was noted earlier (Chapter 5 above) about the high ratio of non-agricultural employment in the total labour force. The survey results show that the agricultural labour force represents only 55 per cent of the rural labour force, i.e. 45 per cent are engaged in non-agricultural activities. This is not surprising and could be explained in terms of the adaptation of a rural population to a situation where the pressure on the very limited supply of arable land is so great and the opportunities for employment in the urban areas are so limited that people have to seek employment of some sort in the countryside itself.[3] Thus, the successive population censuses have shown a growing percentage of the rural labour force in non-agricultural activities. A recent survey of non-farm employment has shown that for 15 developing countries where recent statistics were available, the percentage of the rural labour force primarily engaged in non-farm work was between 30 to 40 per cent and was in fact rising.[4]

Table 6.2 throws some light on the occupational structure of the rural labour force. it is clear that agriculture provides 55 per cent of total employment, with the government and the military accounting for 16 per cent, which makes them the most prominent employers of the non-agricultural labour force. The rest are engaged in crafts and small-scale industries (7.5 per cent), services (mainly petty trade, 5.4 per cent), and construction (1.8 per cent).

Table 6.2: Structure of Rural Employment

Occupation	No.	% of the Labour Force
Agricultural labour force	883	55.4
(a) farmers	(647)	(40.6)
(b) farm labourers	(236)	(14.8)
Industry and crafts	120	7.5
Construction	29	1.8
Services	86	5.4
Government employment	148	9.3
Military	113	7.0
Others	70	4.4
Disabled	146	9.2
Total labour force	1 595	100.0
Looking for work	30	
Total manpower	1 625	

Employment as a Source of Income

Two major observations about employment and income generation have emerged from our earlier analysis.[5] First, a striking feature of the distribution of income by source was the remarkably high proportion of earnings generated from wage-employment in and outside the rural areas, as Table 6.3 shows.

Table 6.3: Distribution of Rural Income by Source

Sources of Income	Income (£E)	%
Wage-employment	152 992	46.2
Income from assets (including family farm)	161 290	48.6
Remittances	17 402	5.2
Total	331 684	100.0

It is clear that the share of labour income is high (46 per cent of total income), especially for rural Egypt, which is usually regarded as a predominantly peasant-based agrarian society. As indicated previously, this high share of labour income can be explained as partly reflecting the impact of adaptation to population pressure in a land-scarce economy (where difficulty of access to land pushes people to seek earnings from hiring their labour), as well as the growing magnitude of the 'commuting

Table 6.4 Average Income by Occupation of Household Head

Occupation of Household Head	No. of Households	% to Total	No. of Households in Each Income Group				Average Household Income (£E)
			Less than 300.0	300.0-499.9	500.0-999.9	1 000+	
Housewife	74	8.5	53	9	11	1	269
Farmer	318	36.7	119	97	76	26	460
Farm labourer	112	12.9	92	11	8	1	239
Craftsman	60	6.9	28	21	10	1	396
Construction worker	19	2.2	5	12	2	—	370
Service worker	61	7.0	27	21	11	2	413
Government employee	105	12.1	45	30	25	5	446
Others	48	5.5	28	10	9	1	343
Disabled	55	6.3	38	8	7	2	266
Regular army	3	0.3	—	1	2	—	579
National service	9	1.0	—	8	1	—	405
Student	2	0.2	1	1	—	—	250
Total	866	100.0	436	229	162	39	384

rural-urban migrant' phenomenon (where many off-village employees live in the village and commute daily to their work).

The second aspect of the relationship between employment and income generation is related to the differentiating effect on households of the differences in the sources of income. We have observed that, in general, and despite the marked multiplicity of income sources of the households, poor households appeared to rely for the greater part of their income (53 per cent) on wage-employment, while the main source of income for non-poor households was earnings from ownership of assets (which accounted for 53 per cent of total income).[6] Furthermore, income differentials between these two main sources of income are substantial. Table 6.4 shows that the lowest average income per household (£E239) accrues to families headed by farm labourers. By contrast, we find that farmers' households were among the highest income groups (with an average income of £E460). The same conclusion can be reached by looking at the distribution of households by occupation of head and income group. While the majority of farm labourers (82 per cent) fall in the lowest income group (below £E300) and thus could be classified as poor, the majority of owner-operator farmers and government officials belong to higher income groups. This point is confirmed further by a comparison of the average daily earnings for the four sources of income with a clearly identifiable labour input. Data in Table 3.5 above show that the highest return on labour (an average of £E1 a day) was from wage-employment outside the village followed by returns on work on family farm (£E0.98). (It should be remembered, however, that this figure included returns to land and other factors of production.) At the other end of the spectrum was wage-employment on other farms, which yielded only £E0.568. Off-farm employment within the village yielded a return in between these two sources (£E0.776).

The differentiating effect of employment status is further complicated by the fact revealed by our survey that, in general, there seems to be a tendency for the working members of the household to take up the same occupation as the household head. Table 6.5 illustrates this point. Seventy-seven per cent of the labour force in households headed by farmers are farm owner-operators. The overwhelming majority (82 per cent) of the workers in farm labourers' households are working on other farms. And about two-thirds (63 per cent) of the working persons in households headed by a government official also work for the government. The same observation is true of other occupations. It appears, therefore, that there is a strong tendency for various occupations to

Table 6.5 Occupation of Household Members by Occupation of Head

Occupation of Household Members[a]	Occupation of Head												
	House-wife	%	Farmer	%	Farm Labourer	%	Crafts, Services, Con-struction	%	Govern-ment	%	Others[b]	%	Total
Farmer	28	45.2	559	77.1	4	2.2	14	5.5	17	9.8	25	13.0	647
Farm labourer	15	24.2	31	4.3	151	82.1	17	6.6	9	5.2	13	6.7	236
Craftsman	1	1.6	12	1.7	3	1.6	92	35.9	6	3.4	6	3.1	120
Construction worker	1	1.6	2	0.3	—	—	23	9.0	2	1.2	1	0.5	29
Service worker	—	—	7	0.9	—	—	74	28.9	4	2.2	1	0.5	86
Government employee	6	9.7	22	3.0	2	1.1	2	0.8	110	63.2	6	3.1	148
Others	2	3.2	4	0.6	1	0.5	6	2.3	2	1.2	55	28.5	70
Disabled	1	1.6	35	4.8	16	8.7	21	8.2	7	4.0	65	33.7	145
Regular army	1	1.6	9	1.2	—	—	2	0.8	2	1.2	3	1.6	17
National service	7	11.3	44	6.1	7	3.8	5	2.0	15	8.6	18	9.3	96
Total labour force, excluding wives	62	100.0	725	100.0	184	100.0	256	100.0	174	100.0	193	100.0	1 594

Notes: a. Includes household members in the labour force only.
b. Includes: disabled, regular army, conscripts, students and those with unspecified occupation.

'reproduce' themselves. It is difficult to judge, on the basis of a once-and-for-all observation, whether the situation is better or worse than before. We can only conclude that whatever forces were at work for increasing socio-economic mobility in rural Egypt, the work of these forces has been very slow. Nor does one expect drastic changes in the near future given the present situation. The spread of education, the most crucial factor for social mobility, is, as we shall see later, far from even.

Features of the Rural Labour Market

The inability of the rural sector to employ the growing rural population resulted in waves of rural-urban migration after the 1930s. However, with the major cities reaching saturation point, rural-urban migration became a less attractive proposition.[7] Under such circumstances, a growing number of the rural population tried to find a livelihood in non-agricultural activities within the village. This was reflected in an increase in employment in such low-productivity activities as handicrafts and petty trade, which formed 15 per cent of total rural employment in our sample (Table 6.2). This process of 'tertiarisation' has been slowed down by the increasing migration of skilled labour from the rural areas either to replace the urban workers (especially in the construction sector) who emigrated to the oil-producing countries of the Middle East,[8] or to work as farmers in labour-scarce countries such as Iraq and the Sudan. The effect of this movement is reflected in the importance of remittances as a source of income and which, according to our survey, amounted to over 5 per cent of total rural incomes. It should be noted, however, that remittances have increased in importance as a source of rural household income, especially since the later 1970s and early 1980s.

Apart from its income generation, external migration has resulted in a 'tightening' of the rural labour market. It is believed that the migration of adult males led to a change in the household structure. An example of such a change is the emergence of 'housewife-headed' households as an important category. Table 6.5 indicates that 45 per cent of the housewife-headed households were farm owner-operators. Table 6.4 indicates that 72 per cent of such households fell in the lowest income group and that the average income of housewife-headed households was about 13 per cent higher than that of farm labourers. lack of comparable data for earlier periods does not allow a full understanding of the evolution of this change in household structure. However, it is safe to assume that more and more housewives, upon the migration of their husbands, took charge of family affairs.

Table 6.6 provides a summary profile of the employment situation on both the supply and demand sides, covering the civilian labour force in the age groups 12-65 years. Distinction is made between unwaged employment and that obtained through the open market. The bottom section of Table 6.6 indicates that two-thirds of the labour supply comes from the employment of members of the family on the farm. Non-family members of the farm provide the remaining third of labour supply. On the demand side, three-quarters of the employment takes place in the village while the remaining quarter takes place outside the village. Employment in the village is itself divided into 58.9 per cent on own farm and 18.2 per cent off the farm in the village. The top panel in Table 6.6 indicating unwaged employment is identical for supply and demand, with 41.1 per cent of the employment by the members of the family on the farm. Other work carried out on an unwaged basis forms 7.5 per cent of the employment not through the open labour market. Total unwaged employment forms 48.6 per cent of total employment, leaving the other half (51.4 per cent) of employment to be fulfilled by open market operations. Within the open market operations, supply of employment is almost equally divided between the farm family (45.9 per cent) and other rural families (54.1 per cent). The decomposition of supply of employment within each of the components of the open market operations portrays a domination of employment outside the village. Within the village, labour hiring for work on the farm dominates employment off the farm. It is interesting to note that within the village, the farm labour employed off family farm as hired labour on other farms (8.9 per cent) marginally exceeds double the family labour employed off-farm in the village (4.1 per cent). This means that of those remaining in the village more are hired as farm labourers rather than in the informal agricultural sector. One reason for the rise of such a situation is the fact that with the tightening of the rural labour market, farm family members who cannot find gainful employment on their family plots offer their labour for hiring to other farmers. This is a further confirmation of the tendency of reproduction of farming occupation referred to above. Another reason for the predominance of family members supplying their labour services to other farmers is that at crisis times, e.g. severe cotton pest attack in the village, an acute labour shortage develops. If one is in the neighbourhood more help can be extended to one's family rather than in the

Table 6.6 Employment, Days per Year, in ILO Sample Population 12–65 Years, Not Including Wives and Conscripts (per cent)

Supply

not through open labour market	1. Farm labour on family farm	41.1	
	2. Other own work of which:	7.5	
	family labour	0.9	
	non-family labour	6.6	
	3. Total	48.6	
through open labour market	4. Family labour employed off family farm of which:	23.6	45.9
	as hired labour on other farms	8.9	17.3
	off-farm in village	4.1	8.0
	outside village	10.6	20.6
	5. Other rural families of which:	27.8	54.1
	as hired farm labour	8.0	15.5
	off-farm in village	7.5	14.6
	outside village	12.3	24.0
	6. Total	51.4	100.0
	Total rural employment	100.0	
	1. From family labour	65.6	
	2. From other families	34.4	
	Total rural employment	100.0	

Demand

not through open labour market	1. Family labour for family farm	41.1	
	2. Other own work of which:	7.5	
	family labour	0.9	
	non-family labour	6.6	
	3. Total	48.6	
through open labour market	4. Hired farm labour of which:	16.9	32.9
	family labour	8.9	17.3
	non-family labour	8.0	15.6
	5. Off-farm in village of which:	11.6	22.6
	family labour	4.1	8.0
	non-family labour	7.5	14.6
	6. Outside village of which:	22.9	44.5
	family labour	10.6	20.5
	non-family labour	12.3	24.0
	7. Total	51.4	100.0
	Total rural employment	100.0	
	1. In village of which:	77.1	100.0
	on farms	58.9	76.4
	off-farms	18.2	23.6
	2. Outside village	22.9	
	Total rural employment	100.0	

the demand side, the open market operations are formed of 51.4 per cent of the employment divided between hired farm labour in the village and those hired, also in the village, in non-agricultural activities in the ratio of 3:2. Hired farm labour, however, is equally divided between farm family and other family. In the case of the off-farm employment in the village, the ratio of farm family to other family is 1:2. The remaining 45 per cent of the open market operations on the demand side is outside the village with almost equal shares between farm and other family. Hence, 'rural labour market' as such is an ambiguous distinction since a section of this so-called rural labour market includes a portion of the urban labour market. Since the urban labour market is affected by the Arab labour market, it may be argued that the latter also has an indirect effect on the rural labour market.

Work outside the village is based on commuting and/or migration. With the latter posing more difficulties to the labourer, it is believed that commuting would be preferred. The sample survey does not provide information on either forms of labour movement, apart from a somewhat broad notion of commuting. This includes not only daily labour commuters but also those who stay a longer period outside the village without being considered to have left the family for good. This situation applies to conscripts and students in the universities. Comparison between commuters and migrants, although not possible by our survey, would have been beneficial in quatifying the size of the pent-up supply of migrants that would flow to the urban centres if living conditions improved in the cities. Nevertheless, the survey indicates that, largely, commuters belong to the lower income brackets. Based on land size, the percentage of the total number of days worked outside the village was 18 per cent and 20 per cent for land sizes of less the 1 feddan and between 1 feddan and less than 3 feddans respectively. Farm family size also has an effect on the number of days per annum worked by farm family members off the family farm. The survey showed a direct relationship between farm family work off the family farm and farm size up to a household size of twelve members when the relationship is reversed. In the first instance this may not explain the notion of 'locked in' labour on small-size farms. However, in light of the fact that family size is positively correlated to farm size, it follows that as family size decreases so does farm size. Survey results, as indicated, showed that as family size decreases so does farm family work off the family farm. Hence, with a decline in the family size this leads to a decline in farm size (positive correlation) which results in a decline in farm family work off the family farm. The relevant family size to explain the 'locked-in' labour at small size farms is that of less than twelve members.

Hiring of farm labour was also found to depend on both farm and family size. On a per farm family basis, hired labour declined up to a size of less than seven members, remained constant for a household size of seven to ten persons and increased with family size of more than ten members. A breakdown by both family and farm size would be useful in understanding the interaction between the hiring-in and hiring-out of a family and farm size.

Table 6.7: Seasonality of Farm Employment (000 days/year)

Season	Farm Families on Family Farms	Farm Families on Other Farms	Other Families on Farms	All Farm Work
Shitwi	60.5	10.5	10.4	81.5
Seifi	73.7	17.4	16.1	107.2
Nili	73.7	17.4	16.1	23.2
Total	150.1	32.5	29.1	211.8
Shitwi as % of total	40.3	32.4	35.8	38.5

Agricultural production is characterised by its seasonal nature. In Egypt, there are three seasons: *shitwi, seifi* and *nili*. Because of loss of the season's importance after the completion of the High Dam, the nili crops are added to the seifi to form the summer season. Seasonal effects bear their marks on the employment in the rural labour market. Table 6.7 presents the distribution of agricultural employment by season and farm type. The percentage of shitwi farm employment to total crops' employment is used as a measure of seasonality. From the above-mentioned table, seasonality of employment by farm families on family farms is less than that experienced on farms with hired labour. Once again, a breakdown of crop seasons by farm size would be instructive to comprehend the interaction between these two elements. A further benefit would be achieved by adding farm work done by wives and children. This might reduce the seasonal fluctuations and help to clarify the degree of division of agricultural operations by sex and age as well as revealing the degree of rigidity between agricultural work and the male, female and child components of labour inputs. The seasonal nature of both the work off-farm and outside the village is not known due to lack of information. It is guessed, however, that in the case of off-farm work seasonality will be minimal and dependent on the degree by which this off-farm work is related to agricultural activity. Depending on the work itself, work outside the village may have its own seasonal pattern which most likely will be completely unrelated to the seasonal pattern of agricultural production.

Rural Wages

Results of our survey have indicated (Table 6.3) that wages represented 46 per cent of the different sources of income in rural Egypt. This aggregate figure nevertheless conceals large wage differentials between seasons and occupation for both family and hired labour. It should be realised that the class 'other family' is far from being homogeneous, including both ends of the spectrum ranging from unskilled farm labour to higher civil servants.

Three different methods of earning wages in addition to that imputed for family members working on family farms have been revealed by the results of the survey. With respect to the village, information has been obtained on wages of family members working on other farms and in the rural informal sector (off-farm in village) together with the wages derived by family members on their family's farm. Wages derived from working outside the village are also recorded. Table 6.8 gives the

Table 6.8   Average Earnings by Rural Labour (£E/day)

	On Family Farm	Wage Labour				
		On other Farms	Off-farm in Village	Outside Village	All Sources	Total Earnings
Farm Family labour	0.98[a]	0.58	0.69	0.93	0.75	0.94
Other family	—	0.56	0.83	1.06	0.85	0.85
All families	0.98[a]	0.57	0.78	1.00	0.81	0.91

Note: a. Average earnings, i.e. net farm income per day worked on family farm by farm family members.

above-mentioned classification of wage-earnings, and reveals that, for farm family labour, wages for a farm family are 5 per cent higher than the level of wages earned from working outside the village. Since wages of family members on their farms are imputed, it is very hard to derive concrete conclusions from these wage differences. Once entering the wage market, family members can derive wages outside the village which are 62 per cent higher than those earned from working on other farms.

Employment in the village informal sector gives the family members a wage which is 74 per cent lower than that obtained from working outside the village. A breakdown of jobs taken up by the family members in the rural informal sector and outside the village could help identify the difference in the wage earned in these two instances. However, it can be safely concluded that this wage difference stems from the fact that village life can provide the working family member with some fringe benefits which have to be paid for commercially outside the village. Transportation and rent are but two examples. Even with the recent emergence of rented accommodation in the villages, the costs will certainly be nowhere near those levels of rent in urban areas.

Turning now to the category of 'other family', it is immediately apparent that wages derived from employment outside the village are almost double those of working as hired farm labour. Again, the same argument put forward in the case of family members applies with the added qualification that this 'other family' category may include some educated members who derive a higher wage than in the case of family members (see next section for a discussion on education), thus pulling up the overall average wage from employment outside the village. This argument may also be used to explain the fact that wages derived from employment in the rural informal sector are about 50 per cent higher than those earned by working as a hired labourer. Another interesting set of conclusions could be drawn from an inter-family comparison. The category 'other family' earns a higher wage than that of the farm family from employment in both the rural informal sector and outside the village. In the case of working as a hired farm labourer, the farm family member earns more than the member of the 'other family' category. The reason for such a difference could originate from the fact that members of 'other family' may be regarded as unskilled in farming practices if compared to an individual who comes from a family with a farming occupation. 'Other family' members are hired to do jobs that require little skill on a piece-rate basis. Even if the situation arises where the 'other family' member is called upon to do a more skilled job, his limited experience entails a supervision from a more skilled person and this has a price not necessarily in monetary terms but certainly in terms of having to keep an eye on how the 'other family' member is doing the job he has been assigned to do. Such close supervision is not necessary in engaging a farm family member and hence reduces the resources tied up for overlooking how the job is being done. In essence, what we are arguing is that a farm family member is paid a premium of about 4 per cent (representing the difference in wages of a hired farm labourer between the two family categories) to account for his farming skills.

Moving to the other employment categories, it could be argued that skills of a different nature are required and their command by 'other family' members moves this skill premium in their favour. On the whole, average earnings from farm family labour are some 10 per cent higher than those from the 'other family'. The reason behind this is embodied in the fact that the imputed wage of a farm family labour has been included. If, however, all sources of wages are considered, 'other family' average wages are 13 per cent higher than that of farm family labour.

So far, the analysis has concentrated on the *level* of wages earned in the rural areas. We shall now turn to a discussion of rural wage determination. The two components of the rural labour market (i.e. supply and demand) are in themselves three-dimensional. On the one hand there is the labour supplied by the family members working on their family farms, off their family farms and the combination of both. On the other hand there are the casual labourers and finally there exist those types of labour which may be available for certain seasonal operations, exemplified by married women and children. Why is this last type of labour not included in the permanent labour classification? The reason stems from the fact that this season-specific operation is not permanent. Why not then include married women and children under the casual labour category? Again they do not quite fit, as they do not have to be chased around in the market when needed. Thus, this category of labour is physically available on permanent grounds but is not permanently employed. Using a casual classification conflicts with their physical permanency within the household. A number of issues are intermingled here, even at the conceptual level of demand and supply determination. Issues like sex, age and agricultural operation specificity with respect to sex and age, education, and social and cultural beliefs all affect both supply and demand of labour in the rural market. Is this the end of the maze of elements affecting rural labour supply and demand? No: farm size and family size cannot be left out. Supply of rural labour, exemplified in our survey by hiring-out of family labour, i.e. family farm labour working off family farm, is positively correlated to family size (up to twelve members as mentioned earlier) and negatively so to farm size.

On the demand side, as family size decreases, hiring-in of labour falls. This is tantamount to the fact that the smaller the farm size is the more intensive is the use made of family labour (assuming that the farmer is a rational being trying to reduce his cash costs). The question left out here is: where does this intensive use of family labour involve a cash wage payment? If out-of-pocket expenses are incurred to other family members as wages, then it is expected to be less than the open market wage rate. If no wages are paid, then the permanency question surfaces in relation to the notion of income sharing within a rural household producing unit. Results obtained so far do not enable us to disentangle the issues raised so far and they have to be left for further research in this respect.

Returning to labour supply, further issues need clarification. Distinction must be made between paid and unpaid labour. Paid labour takes three forms: permanent, casual and operation-specific. Permanent labour, it could be argued, is paid an average wage which is increased by a 'reserve portion' to secure its availability during the peak. Even this 'reserve portion' could be broken down to a portion which ensures retaining the individual in the agricultural activity, especially at the peak, and another reserve ratio keeping that same individual from taking up a job in the rural informal sector. Casual labour hired on a cash basis is called upon during the peak of demand, i.e. during May and, if need arises, in October. Operation-specific types of labour are those that are highly seasonal. Unpaid labour is supplied by members of the family but could also take the form of reciprocity help from neighbours, a phenomenon not uncommon at the present time.[9]

Education

No attempt is made here to repeat the issues raised in Chapter 5 with respect to access to education as revealed by the survey. Our concern at the moment is to outline how the education system could actually affect the rural labour market. While access to education has become virtually costless as a result of government policy adopting free education for all, in the rural areas families do certainly have to pay a cost for their children's education, since the continuation of schooling involves going to the nearest city, possibly incurring transport and lodging costs. What is more important, however, is that the adoption of certificate pricing as a major factor in wage determination in the public sector, together with the guaranteed employment scheme, have resulted in the diversion of human resources away from the agricultural sector. The notion of reserve wage, as indicated in the last section, also affects the wage rates in the rural labour market. It should be stressed, however, that it is not advocated to drop the provision of education as a social good. What is certainly in need of reform is the differentiation between the returns derived from formal education and those derived from vocational training. More often than not graduates of the Faculty of Agriculture accept a public sector job rather than use their education towards the amelioration of the agricultural production process in their village. The fact that entrance requirements, expressed in high school scoring, are ranked low does not help; rather it results in graduates who have no interest in their education apart from using it as a licence for a secure job.

Concluding Remarks

Employment as a major source of income has been the subject matter of this chapter. The features of the rural market affecting rural wage determination and employment have also been discussed. It is worth noting, however, that employment as an income generator affects the level of rural poverty. The relationship between poverty and income derived from employment has already been covered in Chapter 5. No attempt is made here to repeat these findings.

Notes

1. See, for example, ILO: *Rural employment problems in the United Arab Republic* (Geneva, 1969); B. Hansen: 'Employment and wages in rural Egypt', in *American Economic Review*, June 1969; and Amr Mohie-Eldin: 'Employment problems and policies in Egypt', paper submitted to ILO/ECWA Seminar on Manpower and Employment Planning in the Arab Coiuntries, Beirut, 12-24 May 1975.
2. See Chapter 5 above.
3. See Chapter 3 above.
4. D. Anderson and M. W. Leiserson: *Rural enterprise and non-farm employment*, World Bank Paper (Washington, DC, January 1978), p. 17.
5. See Chapters 3 and 5 above.
6. See Chapter 5, p.117.
7. Samir Radwan and Eddy Lee, 'The State and agrarian change: A case study of Egypt, 1952-77', in D. Ghai *et al., Agrarian systems and rural development* (London, Macmillan, 1979), p. 180.
8. For a general assessment of emigration from Egypt see J. S. Birks and C. A. Sinclair: *Human capital on the Nile: Development and emigration in the Arab Republic*

of Egypt and the Democratic Republic of the Sudan, World Employment Programme Working Papers (WEP 2-26/WP28) (Geneva, ILO, May 1978). For an examination of the impact of migration of construction workers see N. Choucri, R. S. Eckaus and A. Mohie-Eldine: 'Migration and employment in the construction sector: Critical factors in Egyptian development', Cairo University/MIT Technological Planning Programme, October 1978, mimeo. According to the latter paper, some 200,000-250,000 workers (or 46.58 per cent of the total workforce in the sector) have emigrated to Arab countries in 1976 and have had to be replaced either by workers from other activities or new entrants from the rural areas.

9. Article in *Al-Ahram Al Iktissady*, No. 703, Cairo, July 1982, p. 39.

7 Efficiency and Equity in the 1980s

In the preceding chapters we attempted to address ourselves to the question of poverty in rural Egypt. In order to do so, a picture of the rural community in 1977, as provided by our survey, was presented. Results of this survey were used to provide both the qualitative and quantitative analysis of poverty. The profile of poverty was presented in terms of the household and not the individual, since the former was recognised to be the basic income sharing unit. Socio-economic variables were used to distinguish between the characteristics and causes of poverty. This distinction was used only as a means of facilitating the analysis and not to imply mutual exclusiveness between the two mentioned variables. Poverty characteristics were identified in terms of such attributes as food intake, consumption pattern and access to the basic needs of education and housing. Causes of poverty were correlated with such factors as access to employment, asset ownership, sources of income and demographic characteristics. The main observation emerging from the survey results was that the ownership of productive assets and access to employment were the main determinants of poverty.

It is precisely the radical change in these two factors, employment and distribution, that influenced the agrarian structure in the 1980s. The question now is to what extent did these changes affect the picture that emerged from our survey? In order to trace these changes, a brief account will be provided of the performance of agriculture in the 1980s with a view to outlining the major elements of the agrarian question at the present time.

Performance Indicators

By the end of the 1970s, the agricultural sector revealed signs of severe deterioration. The share of agriculture in GDP (at constant 1975 prices) amounted to only 19 per cent in 1981, in comparison with 28 per cent in 1975. Similarly, the share of agriculture in commodity production declined from 53 per cent to 40 per cent during the same period.[2]

Agricultural exports, which constituted about 35 per cent of total cent change)

	1960-74				1974-81			
	Per Capita Demand	Total Demand	Domestic Supply	Demand-Supply Gap	Per Capita Demand	Total Demand	Domestic Supply	Demand-Supply Gap
Basic food commodities:								
Wheat	4.1	6.6	1.8	4.8	3.8	6.4	0.6	5.8
Maize	1.8	4.3	3.7	0.6	3.9	6.4	3.5	2.9
Sugar	2.6	4.8	3.5	1.3	8.9	11.6	2.6	9.0
Beans	-3.2	-0.9	-1.5	0.6	-0.2	2.3	-1.6	3.9
Lentils	-0.3	2.0	1.1	0.9	1.4	3.8	-29.0	32.8
Edible oils	3.6	6.1	1.3	4.8	4.6	7.2	0.6	6.6
Exportable field crops:								
Cotton	1.3	3.7	-0.9	4.6	4.2	6.8	1.8	5.0
Rice	2.4	4.9	2.2	2.7	0.3	2.8	1.5	1.3
Onions (winter)	0.7	1.6	0.8	0.8	2.5	4.9	1.3	3.6
Groundnuts	-3.4	-1.9	-0.3	1.6	2.9	6.1	3.9	2.2
Fruits and vegetables:								
Citrus	5.1	7.3	8.3	-1.0	-0.5	2.0	1.4	0.6
Potatoes	3.7	6.2	5.2	-1.0	5.9	8.5	7.9	0.6
Tomatoes	1.6	4.1	4.1	0.0	2.5	5.1	5.1	0.0
Livestock products:								
Red meat	-1.0	1.2	1.6	-0.4	3.8	6.4	1.8	4.6
Poultry	0.1	2.5	2.5	0.0	7.2	9.9	2.8	7.1
Fish	-2.9	-0.4	-0.6	0.2	10.2	13.0	4.5	8.5
Milk	-0.7	1.7	1.5	0.2	4.9	7.5	1.6	5.9

Source: World Bank: *Arab Republic of Egypt: Issues of trade strategy and investment planning. Report No. 4136, (Washington, DC, 14 January 1983), p. 101.*

Table 7.2: Trade Performance and Self-sufficiency for Principal Agricultural Commodities (exports and imports in thousands of tons; self-sufficiency in domestic supply or per cent of total domestic consumption)

	1960		1974		1981	
	Exports (+) or Imports (−)	Self-sufficiency Ratio	Exports (+) or Imports (−)	Self-sufficiency Ratio	Exports (+) or Imports (−)	Self-sufficiency Ratio
Basic food commodities:						
Wheat	−624	69.8	−3 200	36.8	−5 878	24.8
Rice	+272	143.9	+136	111.2	+25	101.7
Maize	−95	94.0	−338	86.6	−1 300	71.1
Sugar	+42	114.2	−23	96.0	−580	53.2
Beans	+11	100.4	−10	92.5	−90	69.8
Lentils	−2	92.3	−13	81.2	−85	5.6
Edible oils	−6	95.4	−151	49.7	−355	31.6
Other exportable field crops:						
Cotton	+375	400.0	+232	211.0	+165	149.6
Onions	+164	170.0	+104	150.0	+40	117.0
Groundnuts	+3.8	17.2	+7.4	12.6	+7.5	18.0
Livestock products:						
Red meat	−16	94.5	−1	99.7	−125	73.3
Poultry	—	100.0	−1	99.2	−606	62.8
Fish	−7	94.5	−19	92.4	−130	53.6
Milk	−85	94.2	−138	92.5	−1 150	62
Fruits and vegetables:						
Citrus	+20	106.8	+162	120.3	+140	114.0
Potatoes	+91	135.1	+100	118.2	+145	113.6
Tomatoes	+4	100.4	+2	100.1	+3	100.1

Source: World Bank, *Arab Republic of Egypt* p. 103.

merchandise exports in 1974, fell to 13 per cent by 1981. Food imports, as a percentage of total merchandise imports, rose from 22 per cent in 1974 to about 25 per cent in 1981. The overall agricultural trade balance, which showed a surplus of 1 per cent of GDP in 1974, recorded a deficit of 9.3 per cent of GDP in 1981.[3]

A closer look at the performance of the agricultural sector reveals a somewhat disturbing picture. Domestic supply of all basic food commodities has failed to keep pace with the demand of the population. The demand-supply gap of basic food staples recorded an average annual change for the period 1974 to 1981 of 5.8 per cent for wheat, 3.9 per cent for beans and as little as 2.9 per cent for maize. Rice, another food staple as well as an export crop, recorded a demand-supply gap, for the same period, of the order of 1.3 per cent. If this demand-supply is translated into self-sufficiency ratios (domestic supply as a ratio of total domestic consumption) as recorded in Table 7.1 below, it is clearly revealed that the growing food gap has been met by a rapidly increasing import of food commodities and a steady decline of exports of agricultural exportable crops: cotton, rice, onions, groundnuts and citrus (see Table 7.2).

The share of agriculture in total employment has also declined to reach about 42 per cent in 1977; with an annual rate of decline of 1.4 per cent since 1971.[4] This decline is expected to continue in the 1980s as long as the male members of the rural labour force continue to be attracted by opportunities in the urban construction sector or to migrate to oil-rich Arab countries.

Factors Affecting Agricultural Performance

The poor performance of the agricultural sector in the early eighties may be explained in terms of two factors. First, the reorientation, since the mid-1970s, of government policy towards the 'open door' or the liberalisation of the economy in general while retaining a large measure of involvement in the agricultural sector. The open door policy, 'Infitah', brought with it new sources of foreign exchange (remittances of Egyptians working abroad together with returns from tourism, oil export revenues and Suez canal duties), as well as subjecting the domestic market more vigorously to international inflation which followed the boom in oil prices after the 1973 war. The sudden increase in oil revenues in the Arab oil-producing countries accelerated massive investment programmes, particularly in the construction sector. These programmes generated increased demand for labour, most of which had to be imported from labour-surplus countries. High wages acted as a demand pull factor for labour from Egypt and, as mentioned earlier, the rural sector's capacity to provide new employment for the increasing population had been exhausted, and the urban sector failed to employ new entrants to the labour market from the countryside except in construction. Moreover, supply restrictions were eased with the elimination of exit visas after 1974, thus enabling the movement of a large volume of emigrants to the neighbouring Arab oil countries. This development, together with a rapid rate of population increase, led to an increase in the demand for food. Consequently, real wages in agriculture increased.

With the foreign exchange constraint easing, the government was under no real pressure to change its handling of the agricultural sector. The partial and *ad hoc* pricing policies remained in use, leading to a widening in the gap between the components of the multi-tier pricing system, i.e. producer, consumer and trade prices. Control of agricultural production using acreage allotments and compulsory quotas persisted and the procurement system for some crops by the State remained in use. With the acceleration in the urbanisation process, further pressures were exerted on the demand for the urban untargeted basic foodstuffs programme in which commodity prices were subsidised and distributed according to a ration system. The easing pressure on the foreign exchange led the government to resort to imports in an attempt to close the food gap resulting from a deficient domestic supply. Apart from the increase in the absolute volume of food imports reaching £E2,147 million at current prices in 1981, the successive devaluation of the Egyptian pound in 1979 (when the official exchange rate was dropped in favour of the parallel exchange rate) and in 1981 (when the parallel exchange rate itself was adjusted upwards) resulted in an augmentation of the value of food imports. Thus, the food subsidy bill increased from £E1,023 million in 1979 to £E1,703 million in 1981 at current prices.

Elements of the Agrarian Question

The components of the agrarian problem in Egypt manifest themselves in a limited (and in fact declining) cultivable area of land, poor water management and a distorted cropping pattern.

Attempts were made to expand the arable land frontier directly by launching an ambitious land reclamation programme, especially during the 1960s. Nevertheless, nearly one-third of the total area of 900,000 feddans reclaimed in the period from 1960-8 was lost due to urbanisation.[5] A number of reasons have been put forward to explain this limited success with reclamation efforts. First, the initial soil studies carried out at the initiation of the reclamation scheme were inadequate. Second, the reclamation work was never adequately finished. Third, irrigation and drainage problems led to shortages of water resulting from breakdowns of the irrigation pumping systems and failure to provide suitable drainage to most of the reclaimed areas. Fourth, reclamation operations were suspended in the face of shortage fo funds, especially during the period 1967-75. Fifth, the institutional structure of managing the reclaimed land varied between being handed over to a public company or given to a new graduate from the Faculty of Agriculture. Both these forms proved very inefficient in bringing the reclaimed land to a level comparable with the marginal old land. In the face of these problems, the emphasis was taken off land reclamation in the 1970s. By the beginning of the 1980s, land reclamation became once more a key element in government development plans.

The increase in the availability of water after the completion of the High Dam has enabled the expansion of the summer cropped area. The inadequacy of the drainage system, coupled with the existing irrigation networks, has resulted in an increase in the volume of the underground water table, leading to an augmentation of the salinity levels in Egyptian soils. It is estimated that about 60 per cent of the total cultivated land in Egypt is significantly affected by problems of drainage.[6] With the construction of the High Dam, availability of water in the irrigation networks has been secured all year round. The existence of this unaltered water works, which is now used in perennial irrigation, only means that a considerable volume of water will seep through soil layers and augment the underground water table. Such seepages are completely independent of the farmer's watering practices or use of the irrigation system.

The cropping pattern which has emerged during the late 1970s and early 1980s is a reflection of the dualistic nature of agricutural production brought about by the government's pricing policy. Agricultural crops could, at the present time, be classified into four main types on the basis of their price structure. At one end of the scale there are the fixed-price crops represented by cotton and sugar cane. At the other end there are those crops such as fruits, vegetables and clover whose prices are determined by market forces. In between these two extremes, there

Table 7.3:   Area of Major Crops: 1960-3, 1970-3 and 1978-81

	1960-3	1970-3	1978-81
Winter crops:			
Full season berseem	690	1 570	1 753
Short season berseem	1 750	1 232	1 013
Wheat	1 387	1 285	1 374
Broad beans	365	292	243
Lentils	78	64	21
Barley	128	82	102
Onions	44	32	22
Fenugreek	55	27	26
Flax	27	29	62
Vegetables	49	179	258
Other	83	87	88
Summer crops:			
Cotton	1 760	1 576	1 182
Rice	791	1 103	997
Maize	271	1 209	1 421
Sorghum	414	462	401
Soya beans	—	2	94
Sesame	45	40	35
Groundnuts	46	36	30
Vegetables	260	348	492
Other	46	86	98
Nili crops:			
Maize	1 456	344	482
Sorghum	55	30	15
Vegetables	138	212	256
Other	18	33	35
Total winter crops	4 750	4 879	4 954
Total summer crops	3 594	5 056	5 000
Total nili crops	1 667	619	718
Orchards	147	251	350
Sugar cane	122	194	250
Total crop area	10 225	10 805	11 092

Source: World Bank, *Arab Republic of Egypt*, p. 108.
Note: Totals include other minor crops.

exist crops which are subject to fixed prices for compulsory quotas with the over-quota balance being sold freely on the market. Such crops include rice, sesame and groundnuts. Further down the scale come wheat and maize, whose prices are affected indirectly via the government's imports and sales.

Classification of crops according to their price structures does not provide a full picture of the cropping system. In a situation of a multiple cropping price, incentives to farmers play an important role in determining the cropping mix. These incentives are of two types: cash and non-cash. Cash incentives take the form of minimising the time that lapses between planting the crop and its sale and finally maximising the volume of crop marketed free of compulsory quota once enough provision has been set aside for on-farm consumption of both food and feed. Cash incentives are directly related to the freedom of prices, while non-cash objectives help to offset some of the effects experienced by cultivators of fixed and quasi-fixed price crops.

The cropping pattern for the periods 1970-3 and 1978-81 conforms to the above-mentioned frame of reference. To devote areas to vegetables and orchards, by the sizeable investment required before the trees bear fruits, is an option open only to large farmers. Vegetables, being labour-intensive, have suffered from rising labour costs and are also limited by proximity to markets in the urban centres. Long clover, with its free prices as well as substantial cash and non-cash incentives, has experienced an acreage increase of 12 per cent. Maize serves as a dual-purpose crop. Maize grains used for human consumption are reinforced by the use of the crop's green leaves as a substitute for scarce green fodder during the summer. The area devoted to maize has increased by about 18 per cent during the same period. While indirectly controlled by the government, the increase in wheat acreage has been enhanced by the increase in straw value as a component of feed.[7] In the case of rice, acreage has recorded a decline of about 10 per cent as a result of high competition from the more profitable maize. Sugar cane, although controlled by the State, has witnessed an increase in its acreage by about 29 per cent. This is the result of the increase in the availability of summer water in the Governorates of Minya, Qena and Aswan. In the case of cotton, whose price and marketing are under complete control of the State, acreage has declined by 25 per cent in the period from 1970-3 to 1978-81.

The avoidance of cotton cultivation by Egyptian farmers has been attributed to its low profitability. While this may be a valid cause, it can yet be argued that there is more to it. The cultivation of cotton seems to be associated with a 'cotton debt syndrome' which the farmer attempts to avoid as much as possible. Given its fixed low price, cash incentives in the form of the maximisation of cash returns are not possible. Being a labour-intensive crop, and in the face of rising labour costs, the minimisation of cash costs becomes a difficult task. Given the small farmer's limited liquidity, he applies for a credit to cover the crop production cost from the co-operative. The value of this credit, together with other services requested for cotton cultivation, are entered against the farmer's account. Cotton occupies the fields for about eight months before it can be harvested. When he is given his cotton seed, the farmer is paid an advance, and the final payment, after deductions for debts, is made after ginning. This results in a cumulative debt formation with the co-operative. It is only the cotton crop which exposes the farmer to this complete cycle, since in the case of other crops the over-quota balance can provide the farmer with direct cash away from the control of the co-operative. Thus, it would not be irrational to avoid cotton cultivation if by doing so the payment of co-operative debts could be postponed or even avoided together with moving on to a more rewarding crop. The possiblility of even a secondary benefit from cotton could not be derived (along the lines of wheat straw) since cottonseed cake is a manufactured product and hence unavailable directly to the farmer on his farm.

Some Concluding Remarks

The performance of Egyptian agriculture outlined above raises a number of issues that bear on the future of that sector.

On the one hand, Egypt is endowed with unbalanced resources: a limited and even declining arable area in the face of a continuously growing population and urban expansion. Demands on the agricultural sector are increasing while output is decreasing and the gap is widening. On the other hand, the agrarian structure operates within a set governmental agrarian policy, a policy which was devised piecemeal and thus has not been able to address effectively the encountered sectoral constraints, let alone face the challenges of the 1980s.

The government's agricultural policy, like most other policies, attempted to tackle the two fundamental issues of equity and efficiency. Value judgements on the performance of the agrarian policy will not add to our understanding of the situation. What is more instructive is to try to analyse how this state policy has tried to accomplish its declared aims and the tools used to meet these ends.

From the start, the agrarian policy gave more weight to equity considerations while assuming that this would not jeopardise efficiency considerations. Equity objectives were to be accomplished by a variety of means. The unequal distribution of the land resources was handled with the proclamation of the agrarian reform. The provision of goods and services was to operate under State directives through a consumer subsidy programme. Efficiency in the allocation of resources was attempted by mandatory rules of production. Acreage allotments, compulsory quotas and consolidation schemes were all used to attempt to direct agricultural resources in the direction of the government's overall development plans. The State perceived a minor role for prices in influencing output. Production decisions were seen by the administration as being independent of prices since allocation of resources was already set by the State directives.

This agricultural policy, set in the 1960s, had to face the challenge of growing demand resulting from increasing population. The initial round of gains began to fade away and by the early seventies the problem re-emerged in a more acute form. Shortages were patched with *ad hoc* decisions. No fundamental changes in agricultural policy were put forward and its rationale was not questioned. The administered pricing system became regressive, leading to a more inequitable distribution, and was reinforced by State directives. The developments of the mid-1970s on the national (open door policy), Arab (oil price boom) and international scenes magnified the challenge. More demand was placed on the sector, which suffered from shrinking resources (land and migrating labour) as a result of a change in the income distribution and consumption patterns in favour of land-intensive products (meat and food).

A pricing system was used which became regressive and production incentives were distorted. A shift took place, as indicated earlier, in land resources, diverting them away from traditional agricultural cash crops in favour of orchards, fodder and vegetables. In addition, the allocative flexibility of land resources resulted in a deterioration of the income differentials, favouring the large and medium sized farmers capable of diversification, leaving the small peasant locked in the 'traditional cash crop trap'.

In sum, the adopted agrarian policy did not completely succeed in reducing inequalities; the distribution of land was not radically changed and the access of the landless to land did not increase. Their sources of income remained restricted to labour income. Migration to Arab oil-producing countries might have helped some farmers, but it has also worsened the situation of the great majority of the rural population. A growing rate of inflation found its way to the countryside via its effect on the cost of living, which is not serviced by the urban-based consumer subsidy programme.

The agrarian system is in need of speedy reform if it is to overcome existing problems and cope with future demands. At the top of the reform priority list is the agricultural pricing policy. The confusion of the role of prices in planning agricultural production needs to be avoided if greater efficiency is to be achieved. Producers' incentives via the price mechanism should not be overlooked. Emphasis should be placed on the allocative function of prices for producers. Distributional questions as they pertain to consumers are another issue. Hence, producer prices should not be depressed, as this will lead to inefficient production outcomes. Consumer prices, however, should be used with distributional considerations in mind and may be handled by lowering consumer prices. Financing the gap between the two sets of prices becomes a government concern and sources of financing this gap should be sought in the fiscal policies at the disposal of the State. The inefficiency of the taxation system should not be used as a valid reason for seeking an easy solution to eliminating the allocative function of producer prices. Such easy solutions only result in further problems and require more government legislation in the pricing and allocational sphere of agricultural production.

Closely related to the problem of agricultural pricing policy is the issue of land taxes. Taxation of agricultural land has been by far the most neglected issue in Egyptian agriculture. In recent years, land tax has been under discussion and some attempts have been put forward to raise its level or at least bring it into effective existence. Land taxes based on a reassessment of the market rentals of land have been suggested. The imposition of this tax on the basis of a realistic assessment of the present-day value of the produce of land would result in a budget revenue which can be used to finance the consumer-producer price gap. It would also lead to a re-allocation of income from the large landlords in favour of the small farmers. The issue of having to leave the collection of land taxes unaltered due to the shortage of administrative machinery should not be used to delay such a reform.

Notes

1. For a detailed discussion of the agrarian question and policies in the 1980s see B. Hansen and S. Radwan: *Employment opportunities and equity in a changing economy: Egypt in the 1980s: A labour market approach* (Geneva, ILO, 1982); and A. Richards and P. L. Martin: *Migration, mechanization and agricultural labour markets in Egypt* (Boulder, Colorado, Westview Press, 1983).
2. See World Bank: *Arab Republic of Egypt: Issues of trade strategy and investment planning,* Report No. 4136-EGT (Washington, DC, 14 January 1983), p. 409.
3. Ibid.
4. Ibid., p. 407.
5. Ibid., p. 104.
6. Ibid., p. 18.

7. This increase in straw value is such that some observers have indicated that the price of a certain weight of flour is cheaper than an equivalent weight of straw or bran and that this has resulted in producers starting to use wheat and its products in feeding livestock and poultry. Dr Y. Wally: 'Strategy of agricultural development in the eighties', Arab Republic of Egypt, Ministry of Agriculture and Food Security, unpublished report, no date.

Index

Page numbers in italics refer to Tables

*For Product Safety Concerns and Information please contact
our EU representative GPSR@taylorandfrancis.com Taylor & Francis
Verlag GmbH, Kaufingerstraße 24, 80331 München, Germany*

T - #0031 - 230425 - C0 - 216/138/10 [12] - CB - 9781032322148 - Gloss Lamination